# NATURAL SPELLER

by
**Kathryn Stout, B.S.Ed., M.Ed.**

**Complete for Teaching Grades 1 - 8**

*Including*
Common words which are frequently misspelled
Latin and Greek word parts and spelling words
Word Categories such as Abbreviations, Contractions
Holidays, Homophones, Measurements, and Numbers

**A Reference Guide for Grades 9 - 12**

*Including*
Spelling Rules
Writing Rules
Greek Word Parts with Meanings
Latin Roots with Meanings

*OTHER TITLES BY KATHRYN STOUT*:
*Comprehensive Composition*
*Critical Conditioning*
*Guides to History Plus*
*Maximum Math*
*The Maya*
*Science Scope*
*Teaching Tips and Techniques*

*Audiocassettes:*
*How To Teach Composition*
*Make It Easy on Yourself*
*Math That Makes Sense*
*Teaching Kids to Think*
*Teaching Reading, Spelling, & Critical Thinking*
*Teaching Tips That Really Work*

Current listings and prices available from Design-A-Study at
Web Site: http://www.designastudy.com/
E-mail: kathryn@designastudy.com
Phone/Fax: (302) 998-3889
or write to the address below.

Published by Design-A-Study
408 Victoria Avenue
Wilmington, DE 19804-2124

Cover Design by Ted Karwowski and Richard B. Stout



Printed in the U.S.A.

ISBN 1-891975-00-5

Library of Congress Catalog Card Number: 98-92681

# CONTENTS

## WHY TEACH SPELLING?

**The purpose** of learning to spell is to write and write and write some more without having to stop and check the dictionary every few minutes. Remember, a computer program's spell check is no help if the word being checked is a correct spelling of a real word: *there* used for *their*, for example. When the typed spelling is phonetic but doesn't resemble a real spelling, there may not be any choices for the correction, either. So, despite the increase in use of computers, students will still have a future that, at the very least, requires spelling skills in order to fill out forms by hand and to write notes and messages.

"**Natural**" **spellers** usually need less practice in order to remember a word, but still need practice adding prefixes and suffixes in order to increase their understanding of word meaning. Allow "natural" spellers to move through the spelling lists at a pace suitable to their ability, adding words misspelled in their compositions, and focusing on building skills listed at the end of the word lists. Practice adding prefixes and suffixes, noting how it changes a word, aids in the understanding of new words. Use of the words in the Latin and Greek sections will also **boost vocabulary development.**

**Students struggling** with spelling often try to memorize each word letter by letter. Seen as a random series of letters, it is not surprising that retention of the new word is short lived. *These students can become "natural" spellers with help.* In any area of difficulty, as many senses as possible should be used by the student. Therefore, this spelling program provides lists with sight and sound patterns in common and offers practical suggestions for including touch when a word proves especially troublesome.

## TEACHING SPELLING

**Choose a group of words** and give the student an oral or written pretest to eliminate any already mastered. Those mastered should be used when adding prefixes and suffixes.

**Word lists for each grade are already organized by a sight/sound pattern** to aid long-term retention. A pattern that the student can **SEE and HEAR** is noted at the top of most lists. This reduces the confusion experienced when several words contain a different spelling of the same sound. For example, few, too, blue, and through all share the sound /oo/. By separating those words and placing each on a list with other words that have the same spelling of /oo/, the student can later recall a word by linking it to one he can spell—"Oh, yeah, that was on the list with `blue`—I spell it t-r-u-e."

Because pronunciations may vary slightly, any word on a sight/sound list may be moved if the teacher finds it better suits a different pattern. For example some pronounce again with the *ai* as a long sounding *a*, while others say *uh/gen*/.

Other words are organized **by category**, which, again, can provide a memory link. Struggling students should take any especially troublesome word from its category and combine it with another word with a common sight/sound pattern, as needed. Those listed in the category "Words for Review" have also been added to sight/sound lists at various grade levels since they are commonly misspelled words requiring extra practice. Words listed as **sight words** are included as common words which require special focus.

**Have the student** use the method described in "**How to Study a Word**" during practice. This is especially necessary for any words that do not follow common patterns or rules.

**Point out that every word should be learned by saying it in syllables and focusing on the spelling of each syllable.** First or second grade students can clap to the sound of the two syllable words listed. From third grade on have students write each word in syllables until saying and spelling each syllable has become a habit.

**Words that are misspelled** on compositions even after study, or those that are already identified as "Words for Review," may require special attention. Have the student write the word on an index card, or a paper kept for this special list, highlighting the trouble spot with a highlighter or writing it in a different color [ w **h** e n ]. The student should then practice spelling the word by looking at it, then closing his eyes and spelling it, OR, by writing the word with his finger on his arm or leg or in a tray of corn meal (adding the sense of touch) *while looking at the word* and saying each syllable and letter.

**Require NEAT handwriting** of each word and all spelling assignments. Careless penmanship can cause confusion of the spelling and can sometimes indicate a careless effort and lack of concentration.

**Assign activities** suited to the needs of the student for daily practice with the spelling words. Retention is best when a student concentrates in small, frequent doses. Therefore, spelling words are usually assigned at the beginning of the week, followed by short (15-30 minute) daily assignments and a final test at the end of the week.

Students should **add prefixes and suffixes** to words on each list in order to build skill with rules. Meanings of prefixes and suffixes should be taught at the same time, increasing vocabulary.

**When providing practice with rules**, encourage the student to recognize their usefulness.

Do NOT give exceptions to the rule until the student has had a chance to apply the rule to a number of words. If exceptions are introduced too quickly he is likely to decide rules aren't really helpful—"after all, there are exceptions. . .why bother to remember the rule." And once again he's back to bad habits—trying to memorize a series of random letters.

Encourage each student to use the words in letters, compositions, conversations, or in any other situation that will help him remember the spellings and word meanings.

**Dictate entire sentences** during testing to provide a meaningful context for the word. Unless students have great difficulty with handwriting, the entire sentence should be written.

This provides a more realistic test of memory since the goal is to increase a student's ability to spell words correctly in written work—where he must compose entire sentences.

Use words in your sentences from past lists and from the "Words by Category" lists to provide extra practice. Check for proper use of capitals and punctuation according to the rules already discussed and practiced. Make a note of any difficulties in these areas that may require extra review.

**Keep a list of any misspelled words** from the test and from written work to add to future lists for additional practice.

# HOW TO STUDY A WORD

**LOOK** at the word carefully.

**SAY** the word **DISTINCTLY**. If you are not sure how to pronounce the word, check the phonetic respelling in the dictionary.

**SAY** the word in **SYLLABLES** while you **LOOK** to see how each syllable is spelled.

**THINK**
- How many syllables are there?
- Is there a prefix or suffix?
- What is the root word?
- Is the root word changed when the suffix is added?
- Are all sounds spelled as expected?

**COPY** the word neatly while you **SAY** each syllable.
**UNDERLINE** or **HIGHLIGHT** any trouble spots.

**PICTURE** the word in your mind.
**WRITE** the word from memory as you **SAY** it.

*Go over each step as many times as necessary to make a mental image of the word.*

## MORE HELP

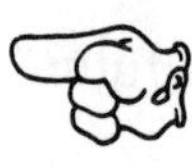

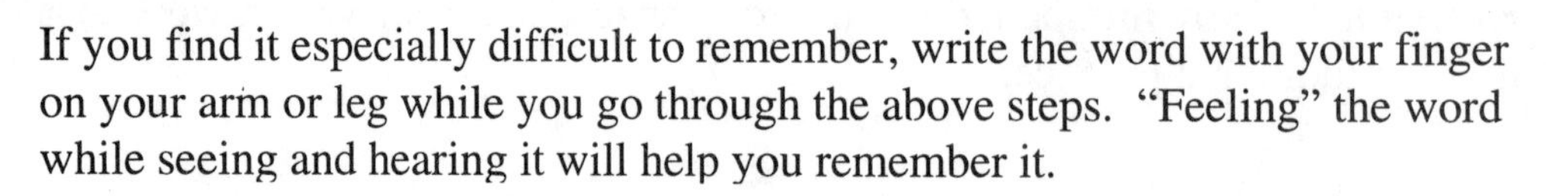

If you find it especially difficult to remember, write the word with your finger on your arm or leg while you go through the above steps. "Feeling" the word while seeing and hearing it will help you remember it.

You can also sing the spelling of a word. Do you remember songs easily? Do you still remember the ABC song? Make up your own simple tunes.

## GRADES 1 - 2

Words for grades one and two are combined to allow for coordination with the phonic program in use. Choose words that the child can already read fluently. It is not necessary to have the same number of words each week—assign from 5 - 10 words. Add to lists by having students add endings to spelling words. Also assign words from "Words by Category" as needed. (Some are listed below for convenience.)

***Sight/sound pattern: one vowel with a short sound***

| *a* | *a* | *a* | *e* | *e* | *e* | *i* | *i* |
|---|---|---|---|---|---|---|---|
| an | bad | mask | red | best | help | in | this |
| and | ask | had | jet | nest | ten | sit | thin |
| ran | hand | sat | bed | let | send | big | with |
| can | stand | last | sled | set | end | it | chip |
| man | black | fast | men | them | step | chin | trip |
| than | at | sad | get | then | next | did | drink |
| plan | that | glad | beg | yes | neck | him | milk |
| am | bat | map | led | test | fresh | if | print |

***Sight/sound pattern: one vowel/ short sound*** ***vowel-r***

| *o* | *o* | *u* | *u* | *ar* | *ar* | *ir* | *or* |
|---|---|---|---|---|---|---|---|
| got | on | sun | such | arm | card | bird | born |
| hop | dog | cut | club | farm | cart | first | more |
| drop | fog | us | much | car | star | girl | for |
| shop | block | fun | cup | far | dark | third | or |
| top | box | run | rub | hard | start | stir | fort |
| not | stop | up | jump | harm | part | shirt | corn |
| hot | mop | but | running | are | apart | birth | horn |

***vowel-consonant-e/long vowel, silent e*** ***end in double consonants that make a single sound***

| *a - e* | *a - e* | *i - e* | *i - e* | *o-e* | | | |
|---|---|---|---|---|---|---|---|
| cake | name | side | time | rose | off | tell | fall |
| take | game | hide | mice | nose | egg | well | call |
| bake | came | ride | five | vote | dull | fell | ball |
| shake | ate | line | white | home | odd | shell | still |
| make | late | mine | nice | hope | doll | smell | will |
| gave | made | shine | like | rode | add | shall | ill |
| cane | same | dine | dime | those | all | hill | bill |

## *Sight/sound pattern:*

| *short i* | *short u* | *end in vowel* | *—s - /z/* | *ends in nk* | *ow says ō* | *aw* | *u-e* |
|---|---|---|---|---|---|---|---|
| mix | trust | do | as | thank | show | saw | tube |
| fix | must | to | has | sank | slow | draw | cube |
| sick | just | who | was | pink | snow | paw | mule |
| pick | luck | two | is | sink | crow | straw | use |
| thick | truck | | his | think | yellow | jaw | used |

| *final y says /ē/* | *end vowel is long* | | *ew says /oo/* | *ow* | *oo says /oo/* | *o says /uh/* |
|---|---|---|---|---|---|---|
| baby | go | fry | blew | now | moon | son |
| many | no | my | grew | how | soon | one |
| happy | so | cry | flew | down | noon | once |
| very | be | try | new | cow | too | come |
| pretty | he | dry | dew | brown | fool | some |
| easy | me | fly | stew | gown | tool | done |
| any | she | by | few | clown | cool | from |
| heavy | we | shy | crew | crown | stool | of |
| | | | | | | love |

| *two vowels make one sound* | | | | | | |
|---|---|---|---|---|---|---|
| *say a* | *ee says e* | *ea say e* | *oo* | *—er/ere* | *—er* | *end in ing* |
| | | | | winter | her | being |
| rain | sleep | clean | room | father | cover | morning |
| sail | green | each | look | sister | never | going |
| train | keep | eat | took | mother | over | thing |
| wait | see | beat | book | brother | helper | string |
| coat | tree | heat | brook | under | farther | bring |
| road | free | meat | good | water | rubber | wing |
| day | three | team | foot | after | river | sting |
| say | bee | read | cook | other | summer | sing |
| stay | meet | east | poor | were | together | swing |

| *Compound Words* | *Sight Words* | | **Calendar Words** *(From "Words by Category")* | |
|---|---|---|---|---|
| today | you | said | Sunday | Thursday |
| into | they | again | Monday | Friday |
| upon | here | the | Tuesday | Saturday |
| inside | put | want | Wednesday | |
| | gone | been | | |

## WORDS BY CATEGORY *continued*

*Add more from lists in the "Words by Category" section as needed. Category words often require frequent review and may be assigned in later grades. *Indicates words in the lists above.*

**Number Words**

| | | | |
|---|---|---|---|
| one | four | seven | ten* |
| two* | five | eight | eleven |
| three* | six | nine | twelve |

**Color Words**

| | | | |
|---|---|---|---|
| black* | yellow* | gray | red* |
| brown* | orange | purple | pink* |
| white* | green* | blue | |

**Homophones**

| | | | |
|---|---|---|---|
| ate* | eight | hear | here* |
| be* | bee* | it's | its |
| buy | by* | meat | meet |
| dear | deer | red* | read |
| four | for* | son | sun |
| hare | hair | tale | tail |

**Contractions**

| | | | |
|---|---|---|---|
| I'll | aren't | doesn't | I've |
| you'll | can't | wasn't | he's |
| we'll | isn't | don't | she's |
| they'll | didn't | hasn't | it's |
| we're | hadn't | let's | I'm |
| they're | won't | o'clock | |

---

## Spelling and Grammar Skills

**Students should practice adding endings to spelling words.**

➧ Practice **spelling rules**: Add endings **s, ing, ed**
*(See "The Rules - Plurals" or "Practicing the Rules" and "Words by Category - Irregular Verbs.")*

➧Notice that some words have meaning as a noun and as a verb.
I take a trip. I take trips. / Don't trip. He trips. He tripped.

**EXAMPLES**

**Add s to make a noun plural:**

| | | | |
|---|---|---|---|
| jet - jets | bed - beds | car - cars | horn - horns |
| map -maps | sled - sleds | truck - trucks | jaw - jaws |

**Add s, ing, ed or use the irregular form of the verb:**

| | | | | |
|---|---|---|---|---|
| bring | brings | bringing | brought | (not bringed) |
| do | does | doing | did | (not doed) (Note rule for adding es to do.) |
| stand | stands | standing | stood | (not standed) |
| bat | bats | batting | batted | (Note rule about doubling the final consonant.) |
| run | runs | running | ran | (not runned) |

**Add s, ing, ed or use the irregular form of the verb:**

| | | | | |
|---|---|---|---|---|
| go | goes | going | went | (not goed) (Note rule for adding es to go.) |
| stir | stirs | stirring | stirred | (Note rule for doubling final consonant) |
| tell | tells | telling | told | (not telled) |
| make | makes | making | made | (not maked) |
| hope | hopes | hoping | hoped | (Note rule for adding ing) |
| plan | plans | planning | planned | (Note rule for doubling final consonant) |

- Practice writing **contractions**. Learn the meaning of the contraction. (I'm - I am) *(See "Words by Category - Contractions.")*

**Students should practice capitalization and punctuation.**

- Practice **writing rules** for capitalization and punctuation: *(See "The Rules - Writing.")*

**Capitalize**

The first word in a sentence
Proper names
Principal words in a title

**Use**

Periods at the end of a sentence.

**Students should practice using a dictionary.**

- Practice **dictionary skills**: *(See "The Rules - Syllables.")*
  - **Alphabetize** by first and second letter.
  - Count **syllables** in a word by listening and clapping to indicate each syllable.

- Practice finding **antonyms** and **synonyms** for spelling words, as possible. (Check a dictionary and/or thesaurus if necessary.)

**Antonyms**

| | | |
|---|---|---|
| hot - cold | bad - good | off - on |
| funny - sad | rise - fall | hard - soft |
| high - low | light - dark | full - empty |
| first - last | more - less | end - begin |
| dull - sharp | fast - slow | inside - outside |

**Synonyms**

| | | |
|---|---|---|
| cent - penny | tell - say | sick - ill |
| stir - mix | end - finish | far - distant |
| beg - plead | fast - quick | fall - drop |
| part - piece | came - arrived | shine - glow |

# GRADE 3

It is not necessary to have the same number of words each week. Assign from 10 - 15 words unless the student has great difficulty with long term retention. In that case assign less than ten, avoiding two different sounds that are spelled the same. (Example: don't give lists with *or* saying /or/ and /er/. ) Add to word lists by having students add endings and prefixes to assigned words. Also use additional words from "Words by Category" as needed. (Some are listed here for convenience.)

***Sight/sound pattern: one vowel/short sound***

| *a* | *e* | *i* | *o* |
|---|---|---|---|
| calf | check | stick | pond |
| half | desk | trick | frog |
| brand | step | twig | frost |
| grand | spend | win | soft |
| plant | spent | lift | ***u*** |
| wash | cent | gift | lunch |
| damp | went | ship | munch |
| camp | rent | dig | crunch |
| past | sent | wish | bunch |
| cast | pest | hid | hunt |
| bath | west | fit | plum |
| clap | chest | witch | crutch |
| walk | bent | pitch | brush |
| talk | wrench | pinch | duck |
| catch | bench | milk | crust |

| *ay-/ā/* | *double consonants* | *ee says/ē* | *ow /ō/* |
|---|---|---|---|
| gray | penny | screen | sow |
| gay | carry | greet | grow |
| way | hurry | street | snow |
| clay | funny | sweet | grown |
| away | sunny | teeth | blow |
| may | cherry | wee | flow |
| fray | marry | sleep | throw |
| pray | hobby | creep | show |
| stray | silly | week | elbow |
| play | jolly | beef | own |
| spray | jelly | feel | thrown |
| holiday | berry | sheep | know |

| ***or - /er/*** | ***word + er*** | ***ought*** | ***oy - /oi/*** |
|---|---|---|---|
| worry | teacher | sought | toy |
| word | worker | bought | boy |
| worth | leader | thought | joy |
| work | farmer | fought | enjoy |
| worm | hunter | brought | employ |

| ***oo*** | ***ure*** | ***—ful*** | ***ear - /er/*** |
|---|---|---|---|
| school | pure | helpful | earth |
| choose | sure | cheerful | learn |
| goose | cure | joyful | earn |
| tooth | surely | tearful | search |

| ***ue - /oo/*** | ***ir*** | ***ur - /er/*** | ***—ire*** |
|---|---|---|---|
| true | thirst | curb | tire |
| blue | dirt | turn | wire |
| glue | first | churn | hire |
| due | birth | burn | fire |
| sue | squirm | curl | tired |
| clue | squirt | hurt | fired |

| ***final silent e*** | ***qu*** | ***Compound Words*** | ***wh—*** |
|---|---|---|---|
| leave | queen | herself | what |
| please | quick | outside | where |
| were | quit | cannot | why |
| none | quilt | anything | when |
| glove | quiet | nothing | while |
| love | queer | something | wheat |

| ***vowel-consonant-e - final e is silent*** | | | ***—ng*** |
|---|---|---|---|
| state | brake | rule | swing |
| space | pine | huge | spring |
| place | price | rude | long |
| face | write | crude | wrong |
| cave | live *(long i)* | tune | young |
| cane | kite | cute | wrong |
| cage | twice | role | hang |
| gate | strike | these | sang |
| trade | prize | eve | lung |

***ar***
yard
yarn
mark
shark
star
start
large
chart
scarf
march
garden

***oi***
coin
oil
spoil
joint
point
join
coil
boil
soil
voice
choice

***double consonant makes one sound***
chess
bless
brass
glass
grass
loss
moss
miss
cliff
sheriff
shall
pull
full
roll
smell
dwell
shell
small
chill
frill
fill
fulfill

***or***
horse
store
shore
short
sailor
flavor
color
actor
neighbor

***—are***
scare
dare
hare
fare
care
share
mare
bare

***Compound Words***
football
baseball
bedroom
railroad
afternoon
within
without
maybe

***Compound Words***
somehow
sometime
somewhere
someone
myself
popcorn
upstairs
birthday

***a—/uh/***
alone
alive
alike
aloud
along
about
around
afraid
awake
asleep
agree
again*
awhile

***ou - /ow/***
out
loud
proud
shout
count
south
mouth
house
mouse
cloud
sound
found
pound
round

***ea - /ē/***
preach
teach
beach
sea
bean
mean
steal
stream
dream
seal
real
heal
deal
beautiful*

***be—***
because
before
beside
begin
belong
below
become
began
between

***silent l***
would
could
should

*(*beautiful does not have a long e sound, but is frequently misspelled. Memory may be helped by adding it to this list and having children exaggerate the pronunciation for spelling purposes only.)*

***ear - /a/***

bear
tear
wear
pear

***al—***

although
always
almost
already

***oo***

hood
stood
wood
wool

***ui***

quilt
built
build
guilt

***silent gh***

sigh
high
flight
tight
light
slight
night
bright
right
fight
sight
might
fright

***ends in er***

number
over
never
later
corner
paper
dinner
bigger
ladder
better
butter
letter
cracker

***end y says ē***

lazy
early
candy
city
only
baby
every
easy*
pony
very*
army
lady
crazy

***ai say ā***

pail
paid
mail
raid
main
strain
sprain
fail
paint
claim
sprain
chain
grain

***Sight Words***

move
does
sugar
field
warm
your
have

***Sight Words***

wash
been
live *(short i)*
whose
bury
great
want*

***u***

put
push
bush
bushes
pushes
bushel
bushy

***au***

caught
taught
fault

**Measurements**

| | |
|---|---|
| dozen | inch |
| cup | foot |
| pint | yard |

***word + ed - doubling***

grabbed
begged
zipped
stepped
dropped
tipped
stopped
mopped

***word + ing***

selling
milking
talking
visiting
bringing
stopping
going
wanting

**Homophones** *(from "Words by Category")*

| | | |
|---|---|---|
| eye | - | I |
| main | - | mane |
| mail | - | male |
| pail | - | pale |
| peak | - | peek |
| sail | - | sale |
| sea | - | see |
| their | there | they're |

*Below are additional excerpts from "Words by Category." Add words as needed.*

**Number Words**

| | | | |
|---|---|---|---|
| first | seventh | thirteen | nineteen |
| second | eighth | fourteen | twenty |
| third | ninth | fifteen | thirty |
| fourth | tenth | sixteen | forty |
| fifth | eleventh | seventeen | fifty |
| sixth | twelfth | eighteen | sixty |

**Contractions**

| | | | |
|---|---|---|---|
| they've | he's | I'd | shouldn't |
| you've | here's | he'd | wouldn't |
| we've | she's | she'd | couldn't |
| they're | that's | you'd | weren't |
| you're | there's | they'd | haven't |
| she'll | who's | there'd | *(See "Words by Category"* |
| he'll | what's | that'd | *for meanings.)* |
| that'll | where's | | |

## Spelling and Grammar Skills

*Refer to the following sections as needed: Activities, Words by Category, The Rules, Teaching Aids*

**Students should practice various forms of a word.**

- Practice **spelling rules**—Add the following endings: s, es, change y to i and add es, change f or fe to ves, ful, est, er (one who), ed (past tense), ing, ly, y.

- Practice adding **prefixes** that change the meaning of a word:
  **un** - meaning "not" **re** - meaning "again"

**EXAMPLES**

*Give the student a list of prefixes and the endings listed above. Have him write the spelling word and additional forms of the word. Use this new list for testing.*

*build* builds rebuild building *(Have the student use building as a noun, also)*
*garden* gardens gardener gardening
*hurry* hurries hurried hurrying unhurried
*turn* turns turned turning return returns returned returning

- Practice **irregular plurals** (child - children) and **irregular verbs** (ran)

- Practice using **apostrophes** to show possession:

  boy's scarf - the scarf of the boy (singular)
  boys' clubhouse - the clubhouse of the boys (plural)

- Practice using and spelling **contractions**, identifying the meaning of the contraction.

- Practice using and spelling **abbreviations**: Mr. Mrs. Miss Dr. a.m. p.m.

- Practice with **homophones** by writing a sentence that indicates the meaning of each homophone, or by choosing the correct spelling when given a sentence.

  The <u>deer</u>/dear stood in the <u>road</u>/rode.

**Students should practice using a dictionary.**

- Practice the following **dictionary skills** (Refer to the sample dictionary page)
  - **Alphabetize** by first, second, and third letter
  - **Turn** to the front (a-g), middle (h-p), or end (q-z) to begin looking for a word.
  - Identify **guide words** and the **entry word**.
  - Match the word to its **dictionary respelling**.
  - Divide the word into **syllables** and mark the accented syllable.
  - Identify **antonyms** and **synonyms**.
  - Use the **pronunciation key**.
  - Recognize that a word has more than one **meaning**.

**Students should practice capitalization and punctuation.**

- Practice the following **writing rules**:

**Capitalize**

I
The first word in a sentence.
Proper names.
Titles.
The first word in each line of poetry.

**Punctuate**

End a sentence with a period, question mark, or exclamation point.
Use a period for certain abbreviations *(See list of abbreviations).*
Use commas.
Use quotation marks.

# GRADE 4

It is not necessary to have the same number of words each week. Assign from 10 - 20 words unless the student has great difficulty with long term retention. In that case, assign less than ten words, avoiding two different sounds of the same spelling in the weekly list (e.g. Don't give lists with gh silent and gh saying /f/). Add frequently misspelled words from the student's compositions. Have students add to their lists by adding prefixes and suffixes. Refer to "Words by Category" for additional words. *Words for review.

***Sight/sound pattern: one vowel/short sound***

***a***

ranch
match
patch
scratch
hatch
track
lack
stack
scrap
tax
lamp
cash
crash
grand
branch

***i***

thick
brick
sick
whip
grin
twin
twist
rich
width
fifth
shrimp
trim
swim
its
which*

***ill***

mill
skill
thrill
grill
pill

***u***

stump
drug
crush
brush

***ung***

hung
rung
stung

***o***

shock
sock
flock
block
stockings
cloth
cost
strong
song
wrong

***a - /ah/***

crawl
palm
calm

***vowel-consonant-e***

throne
whole
stole
tone
stone
lone
smoke

chute
mute
flute
froze
close
hose
chose

***ow***

scowl
frown
growl
brow
crowd
town
owl

***in—***

inside
invent
invite
income
insist
include
inches

***oy - /oi/***

destroy
annoy
voyage

***—en***

open
often
happen

***Compound Words***

newspaper
sidewalk
toothbrush

***Compound Words***

playground
sideways
underwear

***one vowel- long***

kind
mind
find
wind
grind
blind
plight
sign
mild
child
wild

***ank***

thank
drank
blank
sank

***vowel-consonant-e / long a***

fame
blame
shame
frame
tame
lame
safe
scale
male
skate
slate
crate
plane
crane
shave
brave
slave
face
lace
trace
brace
place
race
mate
stage
scrape
craze
case
chase
base

***ar***

rare
scarce

***one vowel - short e***

tend
mend
deck
slept
kept
held
stretch
shed
tenth

***o says /uh/***

won
ton
month
front
son

**—tion**

station
mention
nation
vacation
position
portion
notion
addition
creation
action
fraction
caution

**—er**

cover
daughter
offer
center
anger
finger
flower
wonder
wander
gather
winter
river

**y - /ē/**

navy
gravy
celery
glory
angry
dainty
busy
thirsty
naughty
ugly
sorry
ivory

**o says /ō/**

both
post
ghost
fold
bold
gold
told
sold
cold
hold
old
mold

***gh - /f/***

cough
rough
tough
laugh
enough

***ue says /ū/***

avenue
continue
argue
statue
value

***ea - /eh/***

deaf
sweat
death
breath
ready

***ea - /eh /***

head
read
bread
lead
dead

***oar - /or/***

roar
soar
board
oar

***final le - /l/***

trouble
double
marble
terrible
bubble
pebble
simple
couple
apple
people
steeple
turtle
title
gentle
rifle
middle
riddle
juggle

***final silent e***

raise
praise
strange
range
sleeve
freeze
weave
serve
twelve
geese
charge

***our***

hour
our
flour
sour

***ea - /ē/***

steam
cream
team
scream
beat
heat
meat
least
feast
beast
leaf
peak
speak
reach
season
meal
mean*
jeans

***ai - /ā/***

laid
slain
aid
stain
rain
train
maid
brain
strain
pain
daily

***—less***

helpless
hopeless
careless
fearless

***un—***

unable
until
unusual
unlucky
unfair
unkind
unknown
unlock
unlikely
unhappy
unwilling
unload

***–le***

cattle
battle
little
bottle

***or***

forth
north
torch
porch
order
chore
shore
tore
wore
ignore
visitor

***—ing***

arguing
being
clothing
evening

***a - /uh/***

across
avoid
above
ahead
award
apart
among
apiece
amount
arose
aware
alert

***an***

answer
another
ant
canal

***—al***

central
animal
journal
local
usual
vocal
royal
general
funeral
loyal
annual

| *oa - /ō/* | *ee - /ē/* | *re—* | *Compound Words* |
| --- | --- | --- | --- |
| toast | speed | recover | weekend |
| coach | seek | remember | themselves |
| throat | deed | remind | understand |
| coast | beet | repair | understood |
| coal | sheet | return | whenever |
| soap | sleet | relax | everyone |
| boast | teeth | report | everything |
| roast | heel | remain | everybody |
| loaf | seem | remove | everywhere |
| loan | speech | remark | seashore |

| *—ey* | *2 vowels-r* | *—ar* | *ie - /ī/* |
| --- | --- | --- | --- |
| key | year | dollar | lie |
| monkey | shear | beggar | tie |
| donkey | fear | cellar | untie |
| turkey | tear | collar | cried |
| chimney | court | polar | fried |
| honey | pour | regular | tried |

| *oi* | *—et* | *ow - /ō/* | *Sight Words* |
| --- | --- | --- | --- |
| noisy | market | borrow | shoe |
| noise | basket | shallow | aunt |
| poise | target | narrow | ocean |
| hoist | bucket | follow | friend |
| poison | ticket | tomorrow | vegetable |
| toils | forget | pillow | |

## Words by Category *(Use these and/or other words from "Words by Category" as needed.)*

| **Calendar Words** | | **Measurements** | |
| --- | --- | --- | --- |
| January | August | meter | ounce |
| February | September | centimeter | pound |
| March | October | millimeter | quart |
| April | November | kilometer | gallon |
| May | December | liter | yard |
| June | Christmas | gram | dozen |
| July | Easter | kilogram | teaspoon |

**Homophones**

| | | | | | | | |
|---|---|---|---|---|---|---|---|
| ant* | aunt* | heard | herd | no | know | sale | sail |
| bare | bear | hour | our | plain | plane | sole | soul |
| beat | beet | made | maid | road | rode | some | sum |
| blew | blue | new | knew | sew | so | whole | hole |
| heal | heel | night | knight* | steal | steel | won | one |

## Spelling and Grammar Skills

*Refer to the following sections as needed: Activities, Words by Category, The Rules, Teaching Aids*

**Students should practice various forms of a word.**

- Practice **spelling rules**—Add the following endings: s, es, change y to i and add es, change f or fe to ves, ful, er, est, er and or for "one who", ed (past tense), ing ly, y, less, able, ible, al, en.
  - Practice adding endings to words that require doubling the final consonant before adding endings.
  - Practice adding endings to words ending in y.
- Practice adding **prefixes** that change a word's meaning: **un** and **in** = not **re** = again
  - Check meanings for **affixes** used in spelling words.

**EXAMPLES**

*Give the student a list of prefixes and the endings listed above. Have him write the spelling word and additional forms of the word. Use this new list for testing.*

*breath* breathes breathing breathless
*continue* continues continued continuing continual continually
*forget* forgets forgetting forgot forgotten unforgettable
*heal* heals healed healing
*noise* noises noisy noisier
*reach* reaches reached reaching reachable unreachable
*read* reads reading unread readable
*weave* weaves weaving reweave

- Practice **irregular plurals** and **irregular verbs** correctly.

- Practice using and spelling **contractions**, identifying the meaning of the contraction.

- Practice using and spelling **abbreviations**: Mr. Mrs. Miss Ms. Dr. a.m. p.m.

- Practice writing both singular and plural **possessives**:

  John's keys - the keys of John
  babies' toys - the toys of the babies
  women's dresses - dresses of the women

- Practice with **homophones** by choosing the correct spelling when given a sentence.

  The bear/bare stood in the road/rode.

**Students should practice using a dictionary.**

- Practice the following **dictionary skills** (Refer to the sample dictionary page - p.89)
  - **Alphabetize** by first, second, third, and fourth letter
  - **Turn** to the front (a-g), middle (h-p), or end (q-z) to begin looking for a word.
  - Identify **guide words** and the **entry word**.
  - Read or match the word to its **dictionary respelling**.
  - Divide the word into **syllables** and mark the accented syllable.
  - Identify **antonyms** and **synonyms**.
  - Use the **pronunciation key**.
  - Recognize that a word may have more than one **meaning**.

**Students should practice capitalization and punctuation.**

- Practice all **capitalization rules**.

- Practice proper use of **punctuation**: appropriate end sentence punctuation, commas, and quotation marks.

- Practice identifying and **correcting run-on sentences** with use of punctuation.

- Practice writing using the **friendly letter** format.

# GRADE 5

It is not necessary to have the same number of words each week. Assign from 10 - 20 words unless a student has great difficulty with long term retention. In that case assign ten or less. Add words from "Words by Category" and frequently misspelled words from the student's compositions. Have students add to the assigned list by adding prefixes and suffixes—spelling various forms of each word. (* Review words)
*✦Denotes a word from "Words by Category - French" that has been added to the sight/sound list.*

***say each vowel***

duel
fuel
idea
violet
area
theater

***pre—***

preschool
precook
preheat
prepay
precede
prevent

***ei - /ē/***

receive
perceive
ceiling
neither
either
weird

***ll and ff***

stroll
stall
cell
bluff
stuff
staff

***—age***

courage
damage
savage
village
average
garage
cabbage
message
garbage
language
encourage
percentage

***—en***

kitten
mitten
linen
sudden
frozen
chosen
kitchen
stolen
listen
oxen
children
kindergarten

***final ty - /tē/***

dirty
empty
duty
forty
party
pity
charity
quality
facility
activity
liberty
property

***—tion***

creation
pollution
invitation
repetition
invention
plantation
instruction
devotion
population
transportation
competition
condition

***final the***

bathe
clothe
breathe
soothe
teethe
loathe

***ey - /ē/***

honey
money
alley
galley
valley
journey
chimney

***pro—***

program
protect
propose
proceed
produce
pronounce
protein

***—ture***

future
picture
nature
mature
venture
mixture
pasture

**ie - /ē/**
relieve
believe
achieve
piece
niece
chief
grief
brief
relief
field*

**—ar**
burglar
popular
similar
calendar
grammar
familiar

**—el**
nickel
angel
level

**Compound Words**
breakfast
forever
outline
tonight
grapefruit
railway
however
warehouse
paperback
household

**—or**
minor
motor
harbor
mirror
junior
tailor
doctor
mayor
professor
calculator

**—on**
lemon
cotton
iron
apron
reason
prison
upon
bacon
melon
pardon
person
lesson

**dis—**
dislike
disuse
disgust
disobey
disorder
distrust
discover
distance
disease
dishonest
disappear
discourage

**—al**
visual
casual
capital
total
metal
formal
several
frugal
equal
mural
hospital
horizontal

**con—**
convict
concern
contain
connect
congress
consent
control
contract
construct
content
constant
congregation

**ear - /ar/**
heart
hearth

**ei - long i**
height
sleight

**oi**
anoint
appoint

**—el**
excel
personnel

**final o**
volcano
potato
tomato
piano
hero
hello
cameo

**—ment**
tournament
document
treatment
payment
apartment
department
management

**—ry**
boundary
February*
library
territory
factory
history
victory

**—ous**
dangerous
jealous
nervous
famous
joyous
precious
conscious

***—le***

triple
twinkle
wrinkle
tickle
freckle
pickle
puzzle
dazzle
eagle
single
jungle
bundle
handle
uncle
circle
cycle
stable
cable
noble
cradle

***ea - /eh/***

health
wealth
thread
breadth

***un—***

unusual
undoubtedly

***ei***

reindeer
reign
vein
veil

***—er***

clever
eager
differ
silver
partner
temper
border
meter
powder
lumber
minister
shoulder
sweater
feather
weather
leather
greater
carpenter
hamburger
passenger

***de—***

define
decide
declare
destroy
degree
deprive
delight
decay

***—ial***

initial
partial
official
special

***silent b***

lamb
climb
limb
comb
bomb
crumb
thumb
dumb
debt
doubt

***—able***

table
sable
able
memorable
reachable
teachable
peaceable
manageable

***re—***

reduce
reform
record
recess
remove
remember
recommend
retrieve

***—ness***

goodness
wilderness
kindness
business

***—et***

hatchet
velvet
helmet
secret
carpet
tablet
closet
market
planet
rocket
pocket
locket
jacket
socket
faucet

***ui - /oo/***

fruit
suit
bruise
cruise

***double consonant***

arrow
attend
attitude
assist
arrange
attack
possess
success

***—ful***

useful
thankful
careful
grateful

***gu—***
guitar
guest
guess
guard
guardian
guide
guidance

***wr—***
wring
wreath
wrap
wrote
wren
wrist
writing

***ou - /oo/***
soup
group
route ✧
coupon ✧
crouton ✧
souvenir ✧
acoustics

***ce - /s/***
prejudice
prince
force
surface
juice
chance
police

***—ant***
valiant
important
peasant
pleasant
elephant
merchant
vacant
significant

***—el***
squirrel
model
channel
chapel
tunnel
model
barrel
caramel

***—sure***
pleasure
treasure
measure
pressure
reassure
insure
leisure
fissure

***in—***
information
industry
intention
inform
interest
intend
invite
increase

***ise - /ize/***
exercise
televise
disguise
advise
surprise

***—ward***
forward
toward
awkward
coward
backward

***sc—***
science
scientific
scene
scent
scenic

***ai***
strain
trail
raisin
vain
waist

***—ect***
select
elect
perfect
subject
neglect
insect
reject

***—ect***
affect
collect
inject
expect
inspect
respect
intersect

***per—***
perfume
perform
percent
perhaps
permit
personal
perfect

***ain - /en/***
fountain
bargain
certain
villain
curtain
mountain
captain

***com—***
coming
company
complete
comfort

***—ply***
apply
supply
reply
multiply

***Compound Words***
handsome
meanwhile
downstairs
lonesome

***ain - /ān/***
complain
entertain
explain
remain

***—ic***

basic
electric
music
traffic
plastic
public
magic
tragic

***ough - /ō/***

though
although

***qu***

quest
question
quarrel
quarter
quartet
quickly
quite
quiet
square
squirm
squire
squid

***final y - /ē/***

mercy
crazy
holy
copy
dairy
diary
colony
enemy
memory
category
treasury
cemetery

***app—***

approach
appear
apparent
appetite
apparatus
approve
approximate
application
appliance
apparel
appeal
appease

## Words by Category *(Use these and/or others as needed.)*

**Homophones**

| | | | |
|---|---|---|---|
| beach | beech | pain | pane |
| board | bored | read | reed |
| capital | capitol | rode | road |
| cell | sell | sense | cents |
| chews | choose | way | weigh |
| die | dye | wait | weight |
| due | dew | wear | where |
| fair | fare | weed | we'd |
| feet | feat | week | weak |
| flour | flower | we've | weave |
| forth | fourth | whose | who's |
| grate | great | witch | which |
| horse | hoarse | would | wood |

**Calendar Words**

Christmas*
Easter*
Halloween
Hanukkah
Independence Day
Thanksgiving
Valentine's Day

**Number Words**

thirteenth
fourteenth
fifteenth
sixteenth
seventeenth
eighteenth
nineteenth
twentieth
twenty-one
twenty-two
seventy
eighty
ninety
hundred
thousand
million
billion
trillion
century
millennium

**Foreign Words: *from or via* Spanish**

| | | | |
|---|---|---|---|
| adobe | canyon | cork | sierra |
| alligator | chocolate | corral | tamale |
| armadillo | cockroach | coyote | tornado |
| barbecue | cocoa | guerrilla | mosquito |
| bonanza | chili | poncho | mustang |

## Spelling and Grammar Skills

*Refer to the following sections as needed: Activities, Words by Category, The Rules, Teaching Aids*

**Students should practice various forms of a word.**

- Practice using spelling rules by adding all endings: all plural forms, ed (past tense), ing, ly, y, er, est, ful, ness, or/er ("one who"), less, able, ible, al, en, ion, ation, ment, ance, ence, ant, ent, ive.

- Add prefixes: **un, in, im** (not); **re** (again); **pro** (for, in place of); **pre** (before).

- Identify the meanings for common **affixes** used in spelling words.

- Practice using **irregular past tense forms**.

- Practice writing both singular and plural **possessives**.
  kitten's string - the string of the kitten    cats' string - the string of the cats

**EXAMPLES**

*Give the student a list of prefixes and the endings listed above. Have him write the spelling word and additional forms of the word, checking his work in a dictionary. Use this new list for testing.*

| | |
|---|---|
| *angel* | angels angelic |
| *appear* | appears appeared appearing appearance reappear |
| *apply* | applies applied applying reapply |
| *assist* | assists assisted assisting assistance assistant |
| *attend* | attends attended attending attendance |
| *collect* | collects collected collecting collection collectable collector |
| *differ* | differs differed differing different difference |
| *health* | healthy healthier unhealthy |
| *hero* | heroes heroic heroically |

*Examples continued:*

| | |
|---|---|
| *perfect* | *(accent on first syllable)* imperfect imperfectly perfectly |
| *perfect* | *(accent on second syllable)* perfects perfected perfecting perfection unperfected perfectible imperfection |
| *perform* | performs performed performing performance |
| *possess* | possesses possessed possessing possessive possession repossess |
| *protect* | protects protected protecting protection protective |
| *question* | questions questioned questionable unquestionable unquestioning |
| *wealth* | wealthy |
| *wrap* | wraps wrapped wrapping rewrap unwrap |

**Students should practice using a dictionary.**

- Practice the following **dictionary skills**:
  - **Alphabetize** through the fifth letter.
  - Identify **entry** word, **guide** words.
  - Read and write **phonetic respellings**.
  - Identify various **meanings** for a word.
  - Use the dictionary **pronunciation key**.
  - Identify **antonyms** and **synonyms**.
  - Write words in **syllables**, marking the accented syllable in each.
  - **Turn** to front, middle, or back to begin looking for a word.
  - Find out the history of a word. (**Etymology**)

**Students should practice capitalization and punctuation.**

- Practice correct usage of all **capitalization** rules in writing.

- Practice correct **punctuation**: commas, quotation marks, avoiding run-on sentences.

- Practice use of a variety of **punctuation** to end sentences:
  period, exclamation point, question mark.

- Practice writing letters using the **friendly letter** format.

# GRADE 6

It is not necessary to have the same number of words each week. Assign from 10 - 20 words unless a student has great difficulty with long term retention. In that case assign ten or less. Add words from "Words by Category" and frequently misspelled words from the student's compositions. Have students add to the assigned list by adding prefixes and suffixes—spelling various forms of each word. (*Review words.)
✦ *"Words by Category - French"* ✿ *"Words by Category - North American Indian"*

***kn—***

knoll
knives
knack
knotty
knead
knuckle
know*
knowledge
knock*
knockout
knapsack

***—ish***

perish
flourish
establish
foolish
publish
punish
English

***ex—***

exchange
example
exact
excite
exclaim
exercise
explore
expect
expert
expense
expose
express
extra
extent
exhaust
exist
except
examine
excellent
experiment

***—al***

typical
chemical
technical
identical
physical
intentional
practical
factual
actual
national
global
verbal
oral
vocal
approval
continual
hospital
political
financial
fundamental

***im—***

important
immediate
impress
imprison
imperfect
impatient
impolite
improve
import
imagine
imitate
imbalance
improvement
impossible
imaginary
immigrant
immature
immense
immobile
immune

***re—***

refuel
return
resist
regard
release
research
result

***—en***

shorten
citizen
token
even
fasten
women
frighten

***one vowel***

swift
switch
print
herb
wept
crept
burst

***final y - /I/***

rely
deny
occupy
notify
verify
satisfy
apply

***ch - /k/***

technique
orchid
orchestra
ache
stomach
choir
chord
chorus
character

***in—***

instant
instruct
increase
include
inquire
instead
innocent
introduce
independent

***—ment***

cement
ailment
movement
argument
arrangement
judgment
requirement
amusement
government

***pre—***

precede
precise
predict
prediction
precaution

***—ide***

divide
provide

***—ary***

vary
contrary
literary
primary
temporary
voluntary
secondary
necessary
honorary
hereditary
dietary
solitary
contemporary

***ary - /ery/***

complimentary
summary

***dē—***

develop
delivery
dessert
defeat
deposit
decent
decline
defense
defend
detach
debate
detail
device
determine
decide
desire

***dē—***

deserve
descend
department
delicious
descent

***—it***

wit
spirit
visit
edit
exhibit
admit
limit
profit
habit

***—or***

senator
bachelor
creditor
janitor
elector
author
error
humor
horror
parlor
terror
victor
sculptor
labor
monitor
advisor

***final y - /ē/***

surgery
grocery
mercury
gloomy
steady
sympathy
quantity

***—on***

treason
salmon
parson
common
button
cannon
dragon

***de—***

destruction
despair
decision
definite
desert
desperate
decade

***sub—***

subject
subway
subtract
submit
subnormal
submarine
subscribe

***—ible***

irresistible
possible
terrible
horrible
legible
eligible
audible
admissible
tangible
edible
responsible

***—er***

quiver
shiver
corner
prefer
refer
confer
buyer
owner
printer
defender
reporter

***dis—***

disappoint
disapprove
distract
disaster
discuss
dismiss
district
dispute
display
distant
distance

***—ion***

onion
auction
cushion
opinion
petition
election
competition
companion
operation
champion
division

***ue - /ū/***

issue
pursue
subdue
due

***—um***

vacuum
linoleum
serum
aluminum

***—ey***

attorney
jockey
kidney
parsley

***be—***

believe
beginning
beneath
belittle

***final ō***

soprano
solo
echo
tuxedo
zero
banjo
halo
silo
alto
ratio
patio
studio

***—ence***

intelligence
conscience
patience
obedience
evidence
difference
absence
commence
silence
violence
sentence
coincidence
presence
preference
reference
science*

***—ous***

anxious
curious
vicious
furious
serious
gracious
conscious
precious
spacious
enormous
monstrous
ferocious

***—et***

scarlet
closet
puppet
skillet
bonnet
cabinet
packet
blanket
pamphlet
regret
prophet
covet

***ate - /ut/***

private
delicate

***—an***

human
woman

***ey - /ā/***

convey
survey

***mn***
hymn
solemn
column
autumn

***—ate***
cultivate
appreciate
cooperate
exaggerate

***ou - /ow/***
trousers
drought
blouse
sprout

***—ful***
dreadful
wonderful
awful
beautiful*

***in***
cabin
satin
robin
cousin
basin

***2 vowel sounds***
giant
poem
poet
duet
trio

***—ay***
portray
relay
delay
betray
pray

***un—***
unselfish
uncommon
unknown
unwrap
unaware

***Compound Words***
pastime
overcome
sunset
neighborhood
outfit
limestone
meanwhile
lifeguard
downstream
daylight
nowadays

***final e***
hoarse
coarse
course
nerve
acre
ignore
arrive
athlete
oblige
grieve
solve

***ad—***
admit
advance
admire
adopt
address
adjective
advice
advantage
adventure
adequate
adjust

***—le***
vehicle
struggle
resemble
bicycle
axle
needle
muscle

***—om***
bottom
venom
custom

***—ory***
auditory
directory
laboratory
inventory
satisfactory

***oo***
balloon
raccoon ❂
loose
moose ❂
caboose

***ise - /ize/***
enterprise
advertise
despise
revise
arise

***pro—***
promise
prominent
probably
prospect
prosper

***c - /s/***
pencil
medicine
cylinder
service
source
resource

***ate - /et/***
fortunate
appropriate
associate

***—ous***
miscellaneous
monotonous

***—cient***
ancient
efficient

***—tive***
narrative
positive

***ei - /ee/***
deceive
seize

***ia - two sounds***
burial
cafeteria

| ***—ette*** | ***—geon*** | ***de—*** | ***ou - /ō/*** |
|---|---|---|---|
| barrette ✦ | surgeon | debut ✦ | carousel ✦ |
| silhouette ✦ | pigeon | debris ✦ | limousine ✦ |
| etiquette ✦ | dungeon | deluxe ✦ | camouflage ✦ |
| croquette ✦ | | | |
| cigarette ✦ | | | |

## Words by Category

### *More* Foreign Words from or via French

*(Refer to "Words by Category -French" for spelling patterns and activities.)*

| ***au - /ō/*** | ***qu—*** | ***—gue*** | ***(ou - /oo/ )*** |
|---|---|---|---|
| chauffeur | quality | vague | rouge |
| chauvinist | quail | fatigue | route |
| plateau | quart | intrigue | mousse |
| | | | soufflé |
| ***au*** | ***que - /k/*** | | tourist |
| restaurant | picturesque | | |
| vaudeville | etiquette* *(also on list for "ette")* | | |

### Foreign Words *from* North American Indian

| | | |
|---|---|---|
| chipmunk | opossum | squash |
| hickory | persimmon | squaw |
| moccasin | raccoon | tepee (or teepee) |

### Homophones

| | | | | |
|---|---|---|---|---|
| bin | been | pare | pair | pear |
| break | brake | past | | passed |
| coarse | course | peace | | piece |
| lain | lane | real | | reel |
| lead | led | sent | scent | cent |
| loan | lone | vain | vein | vane |
| might | mite | waste | | waist |

***Refer to pages 62 - 64 for additional homophones, heteronyms, homonyms, and activities.***
***Refer to pages 52 - 61 for word lists using Greek word parts and Latin roots for advanced students.***

## Spelling and Grammar Skills

*See Activities, Words by Category, The Rules, and Teaching Aids for help with the following:*

**Students should practice various forms of a word.**

- Practice using spelling rules by adding all endings: plural forms (s, es, ies), ed, ing, er, est, ful, ness, or/er ("one who"), able, an, en, tion, sion, ment, al, ial, ic, ice, ise, ize, ery, ary, age, ent, ant, ence, ance, ship, hood, y, ly, ous, ive, ity, ate.
- Add prefixes: **un, in, im, re, pro, pre, dis**
- Identify the meanings for common **affixes** used in spelling words.
- Practice using **irregular past tense forms**.
- Practice correct usage of **dye** and **die**, and **lie** and **lay**.
- Practice writing both singular and plural **possessives**.
  kitten's string - the string of the kitten     cats' string - the string of the cats

**EXAMPLES**

*Give the student a list of prefixes and endings (above). Have him write the spelling word and additional forms of the word, checking his work in a dictionary. Use this new list for testing.*

*advertise* advertisement advertises advertised advertising
*appreciate* appreciation appreciates appreciating appreciated appreciative unappreciated unappreciative
*curious* curiosity curiously
*desire* desires desired desirable desirably desirous
*develop* develops developed developing development developmental developer developmentally
*difference* different differently indifferent differential differentiate
*disappoint* disappoints disappointed disappointing disappointment
*exaggerate* exaggerates exaggerated exaggerating exaggeration
*exist* exists existed existing existence preexist preexistent preexistence
*frighten* frightens frightened frightening
*grieve* grieves grieved grieving grievous grievously grievance
*imbalance* balance balanced balances balancing unbalanced

*Examples continued:*

| | | | | | | |
|---|---|---|---|---|---|---|
| *patience* | patient | patiently | impatient | impatiently | | |
| *prefer* | prefers | preferred | preferring | preferable | preference | preferential |
| *provide* | provides | provided | providing | provision | providence | providential |
| *refer* | refers | referred | referring | reference | referral | |
| *verbal* | verbalize | nonverbal | verbally | | | |

**Students should practice using a dictionary.**

- **Alphabetize** through any letter.
- Identify and use **entry** and **guide** words.
- Read and use **phonetic respellings**.
- Identify various **meanings** for a word.
- Use the dictionary **pronunciation key**.
- Identify **antonyms** and **synonyms**.
- Write words in **syllables**, marking the accented syllable in each.
- **Turn** to front, middle, or back to begin looking for a word.
- Find out the history of a word. (**Etymology**)
- **Find correct spellings** of a word
- Identify the **part of speech** of a word using a dictionary

**Students should practice capitalization and punctuation.**

- Practice correct usage of all **capitalization** rules in writing.

- Practice correct **punctuation**:
  commas, quotation marks, avoiding run-on sentences.

- Practice use of a variety of **punctuation** to end sentences:
  period, exclamation point, question mark

- Practice writing letters using the **friendly letter** format.

- Practice writing letters using the **business letter** format.

# GRADE 7

*After using these lists, refer to "Words by Category" to assign words from the following lists:* ***Foreign Words****, including* **Greek** *&* **Latin** *lists,* **Homophones, Heteronyms, & Homonyms***, and* ***Words to Review****. Also assign words misspelled in the student's compositions. Have students add affixes to all lists.*

| *en—* | *—ion* | *final y* | *—le* |
| --- | --- | --- | --- |
| ensure | religion | levy | scramble |
| entangle | region | envy | stumble |
| enslave | portion | fancy | mantle |
| ennoble | collection | mercy | cripple |
| encode | organization | misery | paddle |
| enlighten | civilization | dreary | puddle |
| endanger | imagination | policy | icicle |
| enrich | classification | theory | angle |
| entire | foundation | greedy | triangle |
| engine | occupation | battery | article |
| entertain | description | inquiry | ankle |
| envelope | location | salary | struggle |
| endure | position | ordinary | smuggle |
| entrance | operation | remedy | scrabble |
| engage | digestion | hearty | juvenile |
| enlarge | mention | stingy | tackle |
| environment | disposition | wholly | settle |
| enable | connection | chemistry | vehicle |

| *—al* | *—ty* | *ex—* | *—th* |
| --- | --- | --- | --- |
| electrical | opportunity | exclude | truth |
| nautical | personality | excel | faith |
| mammal | quantity | expand | youth |
| original | ability | exude | birth |
| local | majority | extract | width |
| dismal | immunity | exceed | myth |
| legal | validity | exhaust | worth |
| mental | property | exhilarated | twelfth* |
| official | community | exhaustion | length |
| artificial | society | exhale | strength |
| criminal | variety | exterior | growth |

***—gue***
dialogue
monologue
intrigue
fatigue
vague
league
tongue

***final ō***
stereo
rodeo
echo
buffalo
tobacco
mosquito
tornado

***—ire***
perspire
umpire
empire
retire
hire
inquire
admire

***—ish***
varnish
vanish
abolish
astonish
establish
accomplish
furnish

***—ic***
critic
lyric
comic
critic
specific

***/ō/—***
odor
occasion
obey
obedience

***o - /ah/***
opposite
optical
obligate
option

***ea - /eh/***
sergeant
pageant
weapon
dread
cleanse

***ea***
realistic
really
ideal
repeat
plead
release
lease
conceal

***ie - /e/***
priest
belief
relief
brief
briefly
siege
shriek
handkerchief

***dis—***
discern
disgust
discount
district
discard
disposal
disappear
disease

***mis—***
mistreat
mismatch
misspelled
mistaken
misfortune
misbehave
misunderstood
mispronounce

***—ate***
investigate
cultivate
graduate
operate
estimate
debate
congratulate

***sy—***
sympathy
symmetry
symbol
syllable
system
syrup
synonym

***in—***
incredible
inanimate
inevitable
informal
insecure
inconsiderate
independent

***non—***
nonfiction
nonsense
nonviolent
nonmetal
nondescript
nonrefundable
nonconformist

***ei - /ā/***
skein
beige
freight

***ie***
view
review
preview

***ei - /eh/***
heifer
forfeit
foreign

***—us***
genius
nauseous
nucleus

| ***ee*** | ***ei*** | ***—ness*** | ***ier*** |
|---|---|---|---|
| pioneer | caffeine | witness | pier |
| engineer | receipt | illness | tier |
| queer | conceit | fitness | pierce |
| fleece | conceive | happiness | hosiery |
| geese | | | |
| succeed | ***o - /uh/*** | ***gu—*** | ***ie*** |
| coffee | occur | guild | yield |
| carefree | opponent | guarantee | wield |

| ***Compound Words*** | ***in—*** | ***—ize*** | ***min—*** |
|---|---|---|---|
| throughout | innocent | realize | minute |
| afterward | inspire | criticize | miniature |
| herewith | intent | civilize | mineral |
| however | increase | organize | ministry |
| therefore | infection | recognize | minimal |
| meanwhile | inflate | emphasize | |
| otherwise | instrument | apologize | ***ac—*** |
| nighttime | institute | | acknowledge |
| midnight | indicate | ***ie*** | acquaintance |
| whenever | interior | mischief | acquire |
| farewell | inferior | kerchief | accumulate |
| gentleman | injury | | accompanied |
| copyright | install | ***—ent*** | accuse |
| headache | insignia | continent | |
| anytime | insomnia | persistent | ***—ar*** |
| anywhere | invalid | obedient | cheddar |
| lifetime | intrude | permanent | peculiar |
| policeman | invade | president | particular |
| | | client | hangar |

## Words by Category - Homophones

| | | | | | |
|---|---|---|---|---|---|
| altar | alter | council | counsel | hale | hail |
| aye | I | currant | current | idol | idle |
| boy | buoy | ewe | you | I'll | aisle |
| chilly | chili | flea | flee | peal | peel |

***Refer to pages 62 - 64 for additional homophones, heteronyms, homonyms, and activities.***
***Refer to pages 52 - 61 for word lists using Greek word parts and Latin roots***

## Spelling and Grammar Skills

*Refer to the following sections as needed: Activities, Words by Category, The Rules, Teaching Aids*

**Students should practice various forms of a word.**

- **Add prefixes**: non, un, in, im, mis, re, pre, dis

- **Add suffixes**: er/or, ful, able, less, er, est, ed, ly, y, al, an, en, ation, tion, sion, ion, ment, ness, ous, ic, hood, ent, ient, le, ence, ance, ive, ise, ice, hood, ary, ery *and all plural and past tense forms and ing.*

*Give the student a list of prefixes and the endings listed above. Have him write the spelling word and additional forms of the word. Use this new list for testing.*

*To add prefixes and suffixes, write the base word then list all forms of the word:*

**list word**: mistreat
**base word**: treat

mistreat
treatment
treatable
untreatable
treated
treats
pretreatment
treaty

**list word**: happiness
**base word**: happy

happiness
happily
unhappy
unhappily
happiest
happier

**EXAMPLES**

| | |
|---|---|
| *alter* | alters altered altering alteration alterations unalterable |
| *civilize* | civilization civilizations civilized uncivilized |
| *conceive* | conceives conceived conceiving conceivable inconceivable |
| *counsel* | counsels counseled counseling counselor |
| *criticize* | critic criticizes criticized criticizing criticism uncritical |
| *ideal* | idealist idealism ideally idealize |
| *idol* | idols idolize idolatry |
| *inferior* | inferiority |
| *install* | installs installed installing reinstall reinstalled |
| *intrude* | intrusion intruder intrudes intruded intruding |

*Examples continued:*

*mercy* merciful unmerciful merciless
*mischief* mischievous
*mispronounce* pronounce pronunciation mispronunciation pronouncing
*religion* religions religious irreligious
*symmetry* symmetrical
*sympathy* sympathetic unsympathetic sympathetically unsympathetically
*system* systems systematic unsystematic
*truth* truths untruth untruths truthful truthfully

- Practice using the meanings of common **affixes** to:
  - Determine the meaning of a word
  - Identify the word as a noun, verb, adjective, or adverb.

**Students should practice using a dictionary.**

- Read and use phonetic respellings and pronunciation key.
- Write the word in syllables, marking accented syllable.
- Identify and use various meanings of a word.
- Identify the history of a word (etymology).
- Identify the part of speech of a word using the dictionary.
- Find, identify and use antonyms and synonyms.

**Students should practice capitalization and punctuation.**

- **Punctuation**: practice correct use of commas, semicolon, colon, and quotation marks

- **Write**: all letter formats
  Friendly Letter
  Business Letter - Format 1
  Business Letter - Format 2

# GRADE 8

*Use the lists below as well as lists from the following sections in "Words by Category:"* ***Foreign Words****, including* ***Greek & Latin*** *lists,* ***Homophones, Heteronyms & Homonyms****, and* ***Words to Review****. Add words misspelled in student compositions. Have students add affixes to all lists.*

***—que***
unique
critique
oblique
antique
grotesque
picturesque

***acc—***
accelerate
accident
access
accept
accessory
accommodate

***ai***
strait
straight
plait
impair
reclaim
detain

***ie***
lieutenant
mischievous
soldier
glacier
hygiene
thieves

***—or***
refrigerator
decorator
professor
illustrator
generator
ancestor
endeavor
inventor
creator
meteor
tailor
juror
interior
alligator
counselor
ambassador
governor

***—ic***
relic
panic
barbaric
economic
pacific
republic
metric
italic
epidemic
academic
cubic
historic
epic
classic
terrific
horrific
characteristic

***Compound Words***
old-fashioned
father-in-law
self-reliant
headquarters
first-born
loudspeaker
landslide
sunset
newsstand
courtroom
loophole
folklore
daydream
markup
withhold
daybreak
roommate

***final y says /ē/***
gypsy
mystery
luxury
energy
comedy
tragedy
tyranny
ecstasy
country
faulty
penalty

***—al***
professional
exceptional
disapproval
incidental

***eu***
feud
neutral
amateur
pasteurize

***sch—***
schedule
schism
scheme
scholar

***—ate***
generate
alleviate
abbreviate
communicate

***—tic***
arctic
fantastic
antiseptic
ecstatic

***rh—***
rhyme
rhythm
rhubarb
rhetoric
rhinoceros

***—on***
cinnamon
luncheon
neon
nylon
rayon

***wr—***
write
written
wrote
wrestle
wrench

***—ous***
dubious
treacherous
boisterous
prosperous
disastrous

***—er***
interpreter
cylinder
voucher
semester
commuter
soccer
supporter
schooner
conquer
further
consider

***—ar***
solar
lunar
linear
nuclear
angular
molecular
sonar

***—ege***
privilege
college

***—al***
rehearsal
cymbal
aerial
crystal
cereal
scandal
federal
natural
signal
moral
corporal

***—ent***
evident
competent
confident
convenient
frequent

***—ly***
sincerely
severely
scarcely
especially

***—ance***
maintenance
ignorance
perseverance
brilliance
abundance
vengeance

***—ary***
sanctuary
arbitrary
customary
necessary
secretary
seminary

***—ity***
vicinity
integrity
insanity
majority
generosity
extremity

***—ence***
influence
innocence
permanence
existence
negligence
evidence

## Words by Category - Homophones

| | | |
|---|---|---|
| pray | prey | |
| presents | presence | |
| principal | principle | |
| ring | wring | |
| rain | reign | rein |
| rung | wrung | |
| seen | scene | |
| serial | cereal | |
| site | cite | sight |
| stationary | stationery | |
| straight | strait | |
| tax | tacks | |
| weather | whether | |
| wholly | holy | |
| Yule | you'll | |

***Refer to pages 62 - 64 for additional homophones, heteronyms, homonyms, and activities.***
***Refer to pages 52 - 61 for word lists using Greek word parts and Latin roots***

## Spelling and Grammar Skills

*Refer to the following sections as needed: Activities, Words by Category, The Rules, Teaching Aids*

**Students should practice various forms of a word.**

- Practice adding **all prefixes and suffixes** and identifying their meanings. Students **should write the base word and then each form of the word**, including words from spelling lists using Greek word parts and Latin roots.

- **Add prefixes**: non, un, in, im, mis, re, pre, dis
- **Add suffixes**: er/or, ful, able, less, er, est, ed, ly, y, al, an, en, ation, tion, sion, ion, ment, ness, ous, ic, hood, ent, ient, le, ence, ance, ive, ise, ice, hood, ary, ery *and all plural and past tense forms and ing.*

**EXAMPLES**

*accept* acceptable unacceptable acceptance accepted
*mystery* mysteries mysterious mysteriously
*panic* panicky panicked panicking panics

- Practice identifying a word as a **noun, verb, adjective,** or **adverb** by noting the affix.

**Students should master dictionary skills.**

- Read and use phonetic respellings and pronunciation key.
- Write the word in syllables, marking accented syllable.
- Identify and use various meanings of a word.
- Identify the history of a word (etymology).
- Identify the part of speech of a word using the dictionary.
- Find, identify and use antonyms and synonyms.

**Students should practice capitalization and punctuation.**

- **Punctuation**: practice correct use of commas, semicolon, colon, and quotation marks.
- **Write**: all letter formats.

**EMPHASIZE**

- Mastering skills already introduced.
- Enriching vocabulary by learning word origins, and the meanings of prefixes and suffixes.

# ACTIVITIES

- Choose activities suited to the needs of the student. Anyone finding spelling difficult may need to use suggestions in General Practice every week with only occasional selections from other areas. Other students may find spelling less tedious if they realize that they are mastering other skills at the same time.

- The number of activities per week varies according to the age and ability of the student. Choose as many as can be completed in the allotted time each day. In general, a typical week would include 4 to 6 practice activities.

- The activity suggestions are written for students. You may have them copy assigned words from the lists and then simply refer to the heading and number to read the activities you want completed. A few selections will require advanced teacher preparation.

- Once a rule is taught, have the student write the prefix or suffix inside the cover or on the first page of his notebook. Then he will have a running list of those to apply to his spelling words each week. The student should look up the rule(s) as necessary, and check his final answers with a dictionary.

## General Practice

1. Keep a spelling notebook: write your spelling list and the date; write and save assignments; have a page to list any words you misspell on tests and a page to list words from reading assignments that you don't know. Write a definition or list antonyms and synonyms to help you remember the meaning of those words.

2. Write a sentence for each spelling word.

3. Practice spelling each word by writing it correctly five times.

4. Write each word in syllables.

5. Write the rule for the pattern used to group the spelling words. List the words under the rule.

6. List each spelling word. Next to each word write all the forms of that word by adding prefixes and suffixes. If your spelling word already has a prefix or suffix, (**un**known) write the base word (know) and put the spelling word in the list of words that come from that base word. If it is a verb, include the past tense form (knew).

**hot**: hotter, hottest
**run**: ran, runs, running
**knife**: knives, knifed
**stage**: stages, staged, staging
**happy**: happily, happier, happiest, happiness, unhappy, unhappily
**communicate**: communication, communicative, communicated, communicating, communicates

## Dictionary Skills

1. Alphabetize the list of spelling words.

2. Next to each spelling word write **f** for front (a-g), **m** for middle (h-p), or **b** for back (q-z) to indicate where in the dictionary you would look for each word. *(grade 3+)*

3. Write each word in syllables. Check the dictionary to be sure you wrote each one correctly. *(grade3+)*

4. Write the word with accented syllables marked. Use the dictionary to correct your work. *(3+)*

5. Write each word in a sentence that will show the reader what the word means—like the example sentence after the definition of a word. *(3+)*

6. List the guide words on the dictionary page where you find the spelling word. *(3+)*

7. Most words have more than one meaning or definition. Write two or three meanings for each spelling word. You may list the spelling words separately and have someone match each word with its correct meanings. (3+)

   play: a. have fun b. drama c. make music

8. Write the dictionary respelling of each word. (The spelling that shows the pronunciation.) *(3+)*

9. Using a list of dictionary respellings of the spelling words, match them to the correctly spelled word. *(4+)*

10. Use the dictionary to find out where the word came from—what language. *(5+)*

11. Use the dictionary to find out the original meaning of a word. (Look at the language it came from and find out its meaning in that language.) *(grade 5+)*

## Grammar Skills

1. Write a question using each spelling word.

2. Make all the nouns mean more than one. That is, make each noun plural.

3. Add ing to each verb. Write each new word in a sentence.

4. Write a sentence for each verb using its past tense form. *(grade 2+)*

5. Write sentences using the possessive form of each noun. *(grade 3+)*

6. Write the plural possessive form of each word. *(3+)*

7. Write each verb and next to it write its present, past and future tense. *(3+)*
   saw: see saw will see

8. Write its part of speech next to each spelling word. Use the dictionary to check your answers. *(3+)*

9. Write a verb phrase (verb plus modifiers) with each verb in the spelling list. *(3+)*
   ran: ran swiftly to the entrance of the cave

10. Write sentences using homophones correctly. *(3+)*

11. Write a prepositional phrase with each verb in the spelling list. *(grade 4+)*
    slid: slid on the ice

12. Write a prepositional phrase with each noun in the spelling list. *(4+)*
    lamp: lamp on the desk

13. Make four columns on your paper and give each a heading: nouns, verbs, adjectives, adverbs. Write each spelling word under the heading that describes its part of speech.

14. List each adjective in the list. Add ly to each if it makes the word an adverb. Check the rules for adding ly correctly.

## Building Vocabulary

1. Write an antonym or phrase that has the opposite meaning of each spelling word. *(2+)*

2. Write a synonym or phrase that has the same meaning as each spelling word. *(2+)*
   fifty: one-half of a hundred

3. Homophones: Draw a silly picture to illustrate the two words that sound alike but are spelled differently. You could draw a pail and color it white: a pale pail. You could draw the vegetable beet being hit: beat the beet. Look at the list of homophones for word pairs.

4. Write the definition of each word. *(grade 2+)*

5. Write sentences to show the various meanings of each word. *(2+)*

6. Make 5 columns on a paper. At the top of each column write one of the following: Sight, Smell, Sound, Taste, Touch. Go through the spelling list and put words under the headings that best describe them. *(You may not be able to use every word.)* *(Grades 1 - 2 have the teacher label columns.)*

| Sight | Smell | Sound | Taste | Touch |
|---|---|---|---|---|
| bed | sour | ring | sour | smooth |

7. Using a list of meanings, match them to the correct spelling word. *(grade 2+)*

8. Write 3 - 5 synonyms or describing words each for 4 spelling words. (You may use a thesaurus.) *(3+)*
   speed: fast, slow, quick, rapid

9. Write the meanings of the prefix, suffix, and root (base word). *(grade 4+)*

10. Use the chart of Greek word parts to make a list of ten words that we use in our language. Write the meaning of each word or write sentences showing their meanings. *(grade 5+)*

## Writing

1. Write a word from the list in a way that illustrates the meaning of the word.

Write a word from the list in a shape that will show its meaning.

2. Use some of your spelling words in a paragraph. Choose any topic. Be sure to check over your work for mistakes before turning it in. (This is called proof-reading.) *(3+)*

3. Proofread your compositions. That is, check it over carefully for spelling and punctuation errors. Use the dictionary to check words when you are uncertain of the correct spelling. *(grade 3+)*

4. Proofread someone else's work for spelling errors. Circle misspelled words for the author to correct. *(grade 3+)*

5. Choose four words from the spelling list. Write three one-word clues for each of these words. Let someone guess which word the clues belong to. *(grade 4+)*

| | | |
|---|---|---|
| *Words* | hamburger (3) elephant (2) | explore (4) graze (1) |
| *Clues* | 1. nick-feed-scrape | 3. meat-sandwich-beef |
| | 2. animal-herbivore- mammal | 4. search-examine-unknown |

6. Choose a noun and a verb from the spelling list and build it into an interesting sentence. Too add words ask: What? How? Where? When? What kind? *(4+)*

7. Use some of your spelling words to write one or more sentences telling where, when, what, how, how much, and what kind. *(grade 4+)*

8. Invent some headlines using some of your spelling words. Remember, a headline is brief. It only uses important words and states information clearly. *(grade 4+)*

# WORDS BY CATEGORY

## Abbreviations

**Titles**

Miss
Mrs.
Ms.
Mr.
Dr.

**Days of the Week**

| | |
|---|---|
| Sun. | Thurs. |
| Mon. | Fri. |
| Tues. | Sat. |
| Wed. | |

**Months of the Year**

| | | |
|---|---|---|
| Jan. | May* | Sept. |
| Feb. | Jun. | Oct. |
| Mar. | Jul. | Nov. |
| Apr. | Aug. | Dec. |

**Sometimes M, but usually not abbreviated.*

**General**

a.m. *or* A.M.
p.m. *or* P.M.
IOU
C.O.D.

## Calendar Words

**Days of the Week**

Sunday
Monday
Tuesday
Wednesday
Thursday
Friday
Saturday

**Months of the Year**

| | |
|---|---|
| January | July |
| February | August |
| March | September |
| April | October |
| May | November |
| June | December |

**Holidays**

Christmas
Easter
Halloween
Independence Day
Thanksgiving
Valentine's Day
Hanukkah (Chanukah)

## Color Words

| | | | | | |
|---|---|---|---|---|---|
| black | blue | yellow | orange | pink | white |
| brown | red | green | purple | gray | violet |

## Contractions

*Verb + n't (not)* *(The apostrophe indicates that something is left out.)*

| | | | |
|---|---|---|---|
| aren't | are not | hasn't | has not |
| can't | can not | haven't | have not |
| couldn't | could not | isn't | is not |
| didn't | did not | shouldn't | should not |
| doesn't | does not | wasn't | was not |
| don't | do not | weren't | were not |
| hadn't | had not | wouldn't | would not |

## Contractions

***Pronouns + Verbs - shortened*** ***(The apostrophe indicates that something is left out.)***

| | | | | |
|---|---|---|---|---|
| I'm | I am | it's | it is | |
| you're | you are | she's | she is | |
| we're | we are | here's | here is | |
| they're | they are | that's | that is, | that has |
| I'll | I will | there's | there is | there has |
| he'll | he will | what's | what is | what has |
| she'll | she will | where's | where is | where has |
| we'll | we will | who's | who is | who has |
| you'll | you will | I'd | I would | |
| they'll | they will | he'd | he would | |
| that'll | that will | she'd | she would | |
| they've | they have | you'd | you would | |
| we've | we have | they'd | they would | |
| you've | you have | there'd | there had | there would |
| he's | he is | that'd | that had | that would |

***Other***

| | | | |
|---|---|---|---|
| let's | let us | o'clock | of the clock |

## Foreign Words

### *from* North American Indian

chipmunk
hickory
moccasin
moose
opossum
persimmon
raccoon
squash
squaw
tepee
or teepee

### *from or via* Spanish

adobe
barbecue
bonanza
canyon
chili
chocolate
cockroach
cocoa
cork
corral
coyote
guerrilla
mustang
potato
poncho
pueblo
ranch
sierra
tamale
tomato
alligator (the lizard)
armadillo (little armed one)
mosquito (little fly)
tornado
tortilla

## *from or via* French

| | |
|---|---|
| *Our spellings from the French:* | **qu** - /kw/ (quiet)  **ch** - /sh/ (machine) |
| *Patterns in French words:* | **/k/** spelled **qu** or **que**<br>vowel combinations **ou, au, ie**<br>**ou** is often in the first syllable<br>**ge** sounds like our **dge** |

**ou - /oo/**
tourist
crouton
route
mousse
soufflé
rouge
souvenir
coupon

**ou - /ō/**
carousel
silhouette
camouflage
limousine

**que - /k/**
picturesque
etiquette

**ette**
barrette
croquette
cigarette

**Words of Interest**
porcelain
dandelion
reservoir
sabotage

**au**
restaurant
vaudeville

**qu - /kw/**
quality
quail
quart

**de–**
debut
deluxe
debris

**gue**
vague
fatigue
intrigue

**au**
chauffeur
chauvinist
plateau

**Activity**

Choose words from one language. Label a paper with the following headings: **Places, Persons, Foods, Animals, Things**. Write each word under the correct heading. Look at the meaning of each word in the dictionary to check your work.

## Greek Word Parts - Grades 7-8+

*Learning the meaning and spelling of Greek word parts enhances both spelling and vocabulary skills.*

| Greek Word Part | Meaning | Words We Use |
|---|---|---|
| agon | contest, struggle | agony |
| an | without | anarchy |
| ana | reversed | anagram |
| ant, anti | against | antibiotics |
| arch | first, beginning | archetype |
| aristo | upper class | aristocracy |
| astro | star | astronomy |
| auto | self | automobile |
| bio | life | biology |
| bol | put, place | symbol |
| chrome | color | chromatic |
| chron, chronos | time | chronology |
| cracy | rule | democracy |
| dia | through, across | diagonal |
| demo | people | democracy |
| derma | skin | endodermis |
| doxa | opinion | paradox |
| eco | environment | ecology |
| em, en | in | embryo |
| etym | word | etymology |
| gamos | marriage | polygamous |
| genes | origin | genealogy |
| geo | earth | geology |
| gon | angles | polygon |
| graph | to write or record | autograph |
| gram | something written | telegram |
| hom | same | homonym |
| hydro | water | hydroponics |
| hypo | under | hypodermic |

| Greek Word Part | Meaning | Words We Use |
|---|---|---|
| logos | reason | logic |
| logy, ology | study of | embryology |
| | | |
| mens, mentis | the mind | mentor |
| metry, meter | measure | geometry |
| micro | small | microfilm |
| mono | one | monochrome |
| myth | legend | mythology |
| | | |
| naut | sea, sailor | astronaut |
| | | |
| oculus | eye | oculist |
| odontos | tooth | orthodontics |
| onym | name | antonym |
| opti, opto | vision | optical |
| orthos | right, straight | orthopedics |
| | | |
| pan | all | pandemic |
| paren | beside | parenthesis |
| pathy, pathos | feeling | empathy |
| ped, pod | foot | pedestrian |
| peri | around | periscope |
| phobia | fear | hydrophobia |
| phono | sound | phonograph |
| photo | light | photograph |
| poly | many | polygraph |
| pseud | false | pseudonym |
| psych, psycho | soul, mind | psychology |
| | | |
| scope | see | telescope |
| syl, sym, syn | with | sympathy |
| | | |
| tele | far, far off | telegram |
| techni | skilled | technician |
| thermo | heat | thermometer |
| typos, typi | type | typical |
| theo | god | theology |
| thesis | idea | antithesis |
| | | |
| zoo | (animal) life | zoology |

Special **Spelling Patterns** in words derived from Greek:

| | |
|---|---|
| **ph** sounds like **/f/** | symphony, sphinx, phone |
| **ch** sounds like **/k/** | chronicle, characterize |
| **y** sounds like **/i/** | enzyme, psychic, hydrants (y = long i) |
| **p - silent** when it precedes a consonant (sometimes): pneumonia, psalm, psychology | |

**Plural Forms (Greek and Latin)**

| Singular form | Plural Form | Examples | |
|---|---|---|---|
| word ends in **sis** | change **i to e** | diagnosis to diagnoses | crisis to crises |
| word ends in **us** | change **us to i** | stimulus to stimuli | radius to radii |
| word ends in **um** | change **um to a** | curriculum to curricula | |

## Spelling Words with Greek Word Parts

**onym**
homonym
synonym
antonym
acronym
pseudonym
anonymous

**phone**
stereophonic
microphone
phonograph
symphony
saxophone
phonics
telephone

**logy/ology**
embryology
archeology
technology
mythology
zoology
pathology
geology

**agon**
octagon
agony
polygon
protagonist
antagonize
agonize
hexagon

**auto**
automobile
automatic
autobiography
autograph
autonomy

**graph**
polygraph
telegraph
autograph
typography
photograph

**chrono**
anachronism
synchronize
chronology
chronic
chronicle

**pathy/pathos**
antipathy
pathetic
sympathy
apathy
empathy

**naut**
nautical
astronaut
aeronautic

**astro**
astrolab
astrology
astronomy

**photo**
telephoto
photography
photosynthesis

**hydro**
hydraulic
hydrant
hydrogen

*Spelling Words with one or more Greek Word Parts continued*

**thesis**
hypothesis
antithesis
thesis
parenthesis

**pan**
pandemic
panacea
panorama
pandemonium

**psycho**
psychotic
psychic
psychology
psychoanalyze

**typos/typi**
typical
typify
prototype
stereotype

**syl/sym/syn**
synthetic
synopsis
syndrome
symbol
syllable

**tele**
television
telepathy
telecast
telescope
televised

**opti/opto**
optometry
optimize
optician
optimum
optimist

**micro**
microfilm
microscope
micrometer
microbiology
microbe

**meter/metry**
meter
diameter
geometry
metric

**ortho**
orthodox
orthodontist
orthopedics
orthoscopic

**gram**
grammar
anagram
telegram
program

**arch**
archetype
archenemy
archeology
archeologist

**therm**
thermometer
thermostat
thermos

**cracy**
democracy
aristocracy
autocracy

**phobia**
agoraphobia
claustrophobia
hydrophobia

**eco**
ecology
ecosystem
economy

**dia**
diagram
diadem
diagonal
dialogue

**derma**
hypodermic
endodermis
dermatology
hypodermic

**bio**
biology
biography
biogenic
biorhythm

**anti**
antibiotics
antipathy
antithesis

**peri**
perimeter
periscope

**theo**
theology
theocracy

**mono**
monochromatic
monogamy

**end in sis**
genesis
crisis

## Activities Using Greek Word Parts

1. Write a word in parts like an addition problem and give the meaning. Use the chart for the Greek words parts. Check the dictionary for parts that are not Greek.

   astro + naut = star sailor　　　　micro + scope = seeing small (things)

2. Write a sentence using the Greek word part for our word.

   There was once a naut who loved the sea and traveled tele and wide.

3. Write a one or two paragraph story using Greek word parts whenever possible. Read it to a friend. Can he figure out the meanings? If two people each write a story, trade and translate each other's work.

The naut traveled tele around the geo. He was a techni naut, and loved the pathy of the wind in his face and the sea paren him.

*Translation:* The sailor traveled far around the earth. He was a skilled sailor, and loved the feeling of the wind in his face and the sea beside him.

4. Choose one Greek word part and use the dictionary to make a list of all the words you can find that use that word part. Example: anti: antibody, antibiotic, antiaircraft

## Latin Roots and Meanings - Grade 7- 8+

| Root | | Meaning |
|---|---|---|
| annu | | year |
| audi | | hear |
| bene | | good, well |
| bi | *(prefix)* | two |
| cent | | hundred |
| com | *(prefix)* | together |
| counter | *(prefix)* | opposite |
| cred | | believe, trust |
| dic, dict | | say, speak |
| duc, duct | | lead |
| fer | | bring, carry |
| grad, gress | | step, degree |
| inter | *(prefix)* | between |
| intra | *(prefix)* | within |
| junct | | join |
| jur, jus | | law or right |
| libr | | book |
| magn | | great, large |
| manu | | hand |
| mire | | wonder |
| mit, miss | | send |
| nomen, nomin | | name |
| ory, ary | *(suffix)* | related to, having the quality of |

| Root | | Meaning |
|---|---|---|
| ped, pod | | foot |
| pel, puls | | to drive, push |
| pend | | weigh, hang |
| persona | | person |
| plic | | twist |
| plore | | cry out |
| port | | carry |
| pose | | put, place |
| pre | *(prefix)* | before |
| pro | *(prefix)* | for, in place of |
| re | *(prefix)* | again |
| scrib, script | | write |
| semi | *(prefix)* | half |
| sent, sens | | feel, think |
| sist | | stand firm |
| spec, spect | | look |
| species | | kind or sort |
| spir | | breathe |
| stru, struct | | build |
| sub | | under |
| super | *(prefix)* | beyond, above |
| tend, tens, tent | | stretch |
| tract | | draw, pull |
| trans | *(prefix)* | across |
| tri | | three |
| uni | | one |
| ven, vent | | come |
| vers, vert | | turn |
| vid, vis | | see |
| voc, vok | | call |
| volv, volut | | turn, roll |

## Spelling Words with a Latin Root - Grades 7-8+

**plic**
applicable
implicate
implication
complicate
complication
replica
duplicate
duplicator
duplicity

**plor**
deplorable
explore
explorer
implore
implored
imploring
exploring
explores
exploration

**struct**
instructive
destructible
destructive
reconstruct
construct
instructor
structure
obstruction
destruction

**dic/dict**
dictionary
diction
dictate
dictator
prediction
predict
indictment
predicament
contradiction

**duc/duct**
introduce
reproduce
deduce
inducement
producer
deduction
induction
reduce
introduction
reproduction
introductory
reduction
production

**inter**
interstate
interval
interrupt
interfere
interject
interview
intercept
interpret
internal
interchange
intermediate
international

**spir**
inspire
inspiration
spirit
spiritual
spire
conspiracy
respiration
aspiration
perspire
expire
respiratory
transpire

**vert/vers**
introvert
convert
revert
extrovert
vertical
divert
inverse
converse
versatile
diverse
reverse

**pend**
appendix
compensation
pendulum
depend
pension
expend
suspend
appendage
dependable
expenditure

**uni**
university
unilateral
universe
unique
uniform
unify
unite
unicorn
union
unity

**port**
report
deport
support
opportunity
reporter
deportation
supportive
supported
reported
portable

**voc**
vocabulary
advocate
evoke
vocal
vocalize
invoke
invocation
vocation
vocalist

**pre**
prehistory
prehistoric
prerecorded
preliminary
prediction
precept
precedence
prejudice
precede
premium
prepare
preamble
predestine
precaution
prevent
predator

**com**
composition
compromise
commission
communicate
commit
combine
commercial
compel
communion
company
companion
committee
compare
competitor
compliment

**mit/miss**
submit
admit
admittance
transmit
transmitter
commit
emit
permit
intermittent
dismiss
permissible
admission
permission
intermission
dismissal
submission
transmission

**re**
republic
recess
revise
research
reunion
reduce
reduction
referendum
respond
resist
reform

**intra**
intramural
intravenous
intrastate

**pel/pulse**
repel
impel
expel
dispel
propel
propeller
impulsive
impulse
repulse
repulsive

**volv/volut**
evolve
revolve
involve
revolt
revolution
involved
involvement
evolution

**tend/tens/tent**
pretend
pretentious
intend
intentional
tendon
tendency
attend
attention
tension
contend

**pose**
dispose
transpose
opposite
posture
imposture
depose
impose
imposition
compose
composition

**junct**
conjunction
junction
injunction
conjunctive

**grad**
gradual
graduate
graduation
graduated

**jus/juris**
perjury
jury
justice

**mire**
admire
miracle
admiration
miraculous

**nom**: nominal nominee nominate

*Spelling Words continued*

**magni**
magnify
magnificent

**cent**
century
centennial

**libr**
library
librarian

**ped**
pedal
pedestrian

**trans**
transfer
transform
translate
transparent
transverse
transport
transparency
translation

**semi**
semiweekly
semiannual
semicircle
semicolon
semifinalist
semiarid
semisweet

**scrib/script**
prescribe
prescription
inscribe
inscription
describe
description
scribble
scribe

**fer**
refer
differ
infer
prefer
confer
inference
circumference
conference

**persona**
personage
personal
personality
personable
personally
personify
person

**bene**
benediction
beneficiary
benevolence
benefactor
benefit
beneficial
benevolent

**vis**
visibility
visionary
visible
vision
visual
visor
vista

**ven**
convene
convention
inventory
invent
invention
venture

**bi**
bimonthly
bisect
biweekly
binoculars
biennial
biannual

**audi**
auditorium
audiovisual
auditory
audit
audience
auditor

**sent/sens**
resent
sentry
sentiment
sensible
sensitive
insensitive

**sist/ist**
insist
resist
insistent
consist
persistence
consistent

**cred**
credible
credit
incredible
credentials

**counter**
counterrevolution
counterclockwise
counterattack
counteract

**species**
specific
special
species
specimen

**tri**
triangle
tripod
Trinity
triplets

*Spelling Words continued*

| tract | super | manu | spec/spect |
|---|---|---|---|
| abstract | superintendent | manufacture | spectacular |
| distract | superficial | manual | inspect |
| extract | superlative | manuscript | inspection |
| retract | supersonic | manually | spectator |
| contract | supervise | manufacturer | spectacle |
| detract | superior | | |

## Activities Using Latin Roots

1. Combine roots from the lists to make at least ten words we use. Write the word parts like an addition problem and give the meanings.
   bi (two) + ped (foot) = biped (two-footed)

2. Over one-third of our words have a Latin origin. Choose one Latin root and find at least three words that contain that root. Root: uni unicycle, unit, university, unify

3. Use the dictionary or encyclopedia to find out what any one of the Roman gods listed below symbolized. Then write a word that came from the name of that god. Is the word's meaning related to the god? Try any of these Roman gods:
   Terr, Volcanus, Terminus, Vesta, Pomona, Ceres

4. Use the list of meanings of Latin roots to help you decide on the meaning of each word below. Use the dictionary to check your answers.

| | | | |
|---|---|---|---|
| nominate | credible | portable | audible |
| visual | scribe | diction | spectacle |
| convene | reverse | insist | transfer |
| manual | biannual | admire | deport |

**Answer Key:** *Activities 1 and 2: Check the lists of example words or the dictionary. For additional meanings of common prefixes and suffixes see "Common Affixes and Their meanings." Form for answers: credible = able to be believed*

*Activity 3: Example words may vary from those listed below. The meanings of the sample words below relate to domain of the god, except for Vesta and vestal. In that case, vestal refers to the virgins who kept the fire burning at the altar of Vesta.*

*Terr = god of earth: terrain, terrace, terrarium*
*Pomona = goddess of fruit: pomegranate, pomander*
*Ceres = goddess of grain: cereal*
*Volcanus = god of destructive fire: volcano, volcanic*
*Terminus = god of boundaries: terminal, terminate*
*Vesta= hearth goddess: vestal (chaste)*

**Homophones** *Same Pronunciation - Different Spelling - Different Meaning*

## Homophones - Grades 1-3

| | | | | | | | |
|---|---|---|---|---|---|---|---|
| ate | eight | hare | hair | mail | male | sale | sail |
| be | bee | hear | here | meat | meet | sea | see |
| by | buy | I | eye | pail | pale | son | sun |
| dear | deer | its | it's | red | read | tail | tale |
| for | four | their there they're | | | | main | mane |

## Homophones - Grades 4-6

| | | | | | | | |
|---|---|---|---|---|---|---|---|
| aunt | ant | blew | blue | chews | choose | feet | feat |
| bare | bear | break | brake | coarse | course | flower | flour |
| beach | beech | board | bored | die | dye | fourth | forth |
| beet | beat | capital | capitol | due | dew | grate | great |
| bin | been | cell | sell | fair | fare | heal | heel |
| heard | herd | lone | loan | no | know | peace | piece |
| hoarse | horse | made | maid | or ore | oar | plane | plain |
| hour | our | might | mite | pain | pane | read | reed |
| lain | lane | new | knew | pare pair | pear | real | reel |
| lead | led | night | knight | past | passed | right | write |
| road | rode | steal | steel | way | weigh | whole | hole |
| sense | cents | sum | some | wear | where | whose | who's |
| sent scent | cent | vein vain | vane | weave | we've | witch | which |
| sew | so | wait | weight | weed | we'd | won | one |
| soul | sole | waste | waist | week | weak | would | wood |

## Homophones - Grades 7-8

| | | | | | | | |
|---|---|---|---|---|---|---|---|
| altar | alter | | council | counsel | | hale | hail |
| aye | I | | currant | current | | idol | idle |
| boy | buoy | | ewe | you | | I'll | aisle |
| chilly | chili | | flea | flee | | peal | peel |

| | | | | |
|---|---|---|---|---|
| pray | | prey | rain reign | rein |
| presents | | presence | rung | wrung |
| principal | | principle | seen | scene |
| ring | | wring | serial | cereal |

| | | | |
|---|---|---|---|
| site cite | sight | weather | whether |
| stationary | stationery | wholly | holy |
| straight | strait | Yule | you'll |
| tax | tacks | | |

## Heteronyms

*Different Pronunciation - Same Spelling - Different Meaning*
*Grade 6 - 8*

- ***Shift the accent from the first to the second syllable:*** **com'** pact com **pact'**

| | | | |
|---|---|---|---|
| compact | convert | export | perfect |
| conduct | convict | extract | permit |
| content | discard | insult | presents |
| contest | entrance | invalid | project |
| contract | excuse | object | recess |
| record | refund | refuse | subject |
| transfer | | | |

- ***Change the final sound from*** **ate** *to* **it**: ap pro pri **ate'** ap **pro'** pri it

| | | | |
|---|---|---|---|
| appropriate | associate | elaborate | approximate |
| duplicate | graduate | separate | |

- ***The i changes from the long sound to the short vowel sound:*** wind wind

## Homonyms

*Same Pronunciation - Same Spelling - Different Meaning*
*Grades 6 - 8*

| | | |
|---|---|---|
| flounder - a fish | low - referring to elevation | squall - a cry |
| flounder - thrash about | low - to moo | squall - a gale |

## Activity

Write the two words. Next to each word write the dictionary respelling if the words are spelled the same but sound different. Choose one of the following to show meaning.

- Write a definition
- Write an example sentence
- Write two synonyms and an antonym
- Draw a picture.

## Irregular Verbs

Regular verbs add ed for past forms: I talk. I talked. Irregular verbs change their spelling, or remain the same. The past participle uses a form of have or be (*has* gone, *was* examined) or modifies nouns and pronouns by itself (*charmed* life). It is usually the same as the past tense form, except in most irregular verbs. Where two forms are possible (dove, dived) both are listed. Below are some of the most common irregular verbs. The dictionary does list irregular forms.

### Grades 3-6

| Present | Past | Past Participle |
|---|---|---|
| become | became | become |
| begin | began | begun |
| blow | blew | blown |
| build | built | built |
| catch | caught | caught |
| choose | chose | chosen |
| come | came | come |
| do | did | done |
| draw | drew | drawn |
| drink | drank | drunk |
| drive | drove | driven |
| eat | ate | eaten |
| fall | fell | fallen |
| fly | flew | flown |
| freeze | froze | frozen |

| Present | Past | Past Participle |
|---|---|---|
| give | gave | given |
| go | went | gone |
| grow | grew | grown |
| make | made | made |
| mean | meant | meant |
| run | ran | run |
| see | saw | seen |
| show | showed | shown |
| speak | spoke | spoken |
| steal | stole | stolen |
| take | took | taken |
| tear | tore | torn |
| thrown | threw | thrown |
| wear | wore | worn |
| write | wrote | written |

### Grades 6-8

| Present | Past | Past Participle |
|---|---|---|
| bear | bore | borne |
| beat | beat | beaten |
| bite | bit | bitten, bit |
| break | broke | broken |
| bring | brought | brought |

| Present | Past | Past Participle |
|---|---|---|
| lose | lost | lost |
| ride | rode | ridden |
| ring | rang | rung |
| rise | rose | risen |
| say | said | said |

*Grades 6-8*

| **Present** | **Past** | **Past Participle** |
|---|---|---|
| burst | burst | burst |
| catch | caught | caught |
| dive | dived, dove | dived |
| hurt | hurt | hurt |
| know | knew | known |
| lay* | laid | laid |
| lead | led | led |
| leave | left | left |
| lend | lent | lent |
| lie** | lay | lain |

**lay - to place* ***lie - to recline or rest*

| **Present** | **Past** | **Past Participle** |
|---|---|---|
| seek | sought | sought |
| set | set | set |
| shake | shook | shaken |
| shine | shone | shone |
| shrink | shrank, shrunk | shrunk, shrunken |
| sing | sang, sung | sung |
| sink | sank | sunk |
| slay | slew | slain |
| spring | sprang, sprung | sprung |
| swim | swam | swum |

## Measurements

| | |
|---|---|
| m | meter |
| cm | centimeter |
| mm | millimeter |
| km | kilometer |
| L | liter |
| g | gram |
| kg | kilogram |

| | |
|---|---|
| oz. | ounce |
| lb. | pound |
| pt. | pint |
| qt. | quart |
| gal. | gallon |
| t *or* tsp. | teaspoon |
| T *or* tbsp. | tablespoon |

| | |
|---|---|
| inch | in. |
| foot | ft. |
| yard | yd. |
| mile | mi. |
| dozen | doz. |

## Number Words

one
two
three
four
five
six
seven
eight
nine
ten
eleven
twelve
thirteen
fourteen
fifteen

sixteen
seventeen
eighteen
nineteen
twenty
twenty-one
twenty-two
thirty
forty
fifty
sixty
seventy
eighty
ninety
one hundred

thousand
million
billion
trillion
century
millennium

first
second
third
fourth
fifth

sixth
seventh
eighth
ninth
tenth
eleventh
twelfth
thirteenth
fourteenth
fifteenth
sixteenth
seventeenth
eighteenth
nineteenth
twentieth

## Words for Review

absence
accept
ache
again
aisle
all right
almost
already
among
angel
angle
another
answer
argue
aunt
away
awful

been
before
beginning
believe
bought
brought
build
business
busy

calendar
caught
chief
children
choose
clothes
cold
color
cough
could

country
course
cousin

different
doctor
does
done
dropped

early
enough

February
foreign
forty
fourth
friend
frightened

goes
grammar
guess

happen
handkerchief
heard
height
here
hole
hour

idea
imagine
its
it's

kept

knew
know

laid
laugh
let's
library
loose
lose

minute
much
muscle

necessary
neighbor
nickel
niece
ninety
ninth

occasion
occurred
occurrence
often
once
opposite

quiet
quit
quite

raise
ready
really
receive
receipt
rhythm

said
school
separate
stationary
sugar
sure
surprise

that's
their
they're
though
tired
together
tough
trouble
truly

until
unusual
used

want
was
weak
wear
weather
Wednesday
weird
where
whether
whole
would
writing
written
wrote
your
you're

# THE RULES

## Spelling Rules

### Consonant Sounds

**Double Consonants**: bb dd gg mm nn pp When the single letter sound is heard in the middle of a two syllable word AND the consonant follows the short sound of vowels **a**, **e**, **i**, **o**, or **u**, write two consonants for one sound. (rabbit, funny)

| Sound | Spelled | When | Example |
|---|---|---|---|
| /ch/ | ch | At the beginning of words | chat |
| /ch/ | ch or tch | At the end of a word | watch |
| /ch/ | t | If t is followed by ure or ion | picture |
| /f/ | ph | In words from Latin or Greek | phone |
| /f/ | gh | In a few words to memorize: cough, enough, rough, laugh, tough | |
| /f/ | ff | In the middle or at the end of some words. | sniff, offer |
| /f/ | f | At the beginning, middle, and/or end of words. | farm |
| /g/ | g | When g is followed by a, o, or u (If the u is followed by another vowel, u is usually silent - guilty) | gate, gone, guard |
| /j/ | g | When g is followed by e, i, or y | page, giant, gym |
| /j/ | dge | At the end of a word after the short sounds of vowels a, e, i, o, or u | edge |
| /k/ | c | Followed by a, o, u, l, or r | club |
| /k/ | ck | Ending a one syllable word after vowels a, e, i, o, u | back, check |
| /k/ | ch | In some words. | chorus, choir |
| /k/ | k | At the beginning of a word before e or i | keep |
| /k/ | que | At the end of some words. | antique |
| /kw/ | qu | In English words u always follows q | quilt |
| /l/ | l | At the beginning of words | later |
| /l/ | l or ll | At the end of words | channel, tell |

| Sound | Spelling | When | Example |
|---|---|---|---|
| /l/ | ll | In the middle of a word when the l sound is between two vowels | collar |
| /m/ | mb | At the end of a few words to memorize: bomb , comb, crumb, dumb, limb, thumb, lamb, climb | |
| /ng/ | ng | At the end of a word (*except* **tongue**) | hang |
| /ng/ | n | Within a word before the sound /k/ | uncle, think |
| /r/ | rr | When between two vowel sounds within a word of more than one syllable | carry |
| /r/ | rh | In a few words to memorize: rhinoceros, rhinestone, rhyme, rhubarb | rhyme |
| /s/ | c | When c is followed by e, i, or y | cent, agency |
| /s/ | s | At the beginning of a syllable | |
| /s/ or /z/ | s or se | At the end of a word | gas, base, has |
| /sh/ | s | When s is followed by ion or ure | decision, sure |
| /sh/ | t | When t is followed by ion (also may be pronounced chun - suggestion) | attention |
| /sh/ | ci | In cial and cious | facial, spacious |
| /sh/ | ti | In tial and tious | partial, fictitious |
| /th/ | th | Except at the end of some words using the | throw, either, truth |
| /th/ | the | Only at the end of a word | bathe, clothe |
| /v/ | v | When followed by another letter. It is never the last letter. | love |

## Vowel Sounds

| Sound | Spelling | When – Example |
|---|---|---|
| short a, e, i, o, u | one letter a, e, i, o, or u | In one-syllable words where the vowel is in the middle: tan, ten, tin, run |
| long sound of first vowel | two vowels together | When two vowels are together, the first is long, the second is silent |
| /ā/ | ai, ay, | aid, say |

*Vowel Sounds continued*

| **Sound** | **Spelling** | **When — Example** |
|---|---|---|
| /ē/ | ea, ee, ei, ey | each, keep, either, donkey |
| Long i | ie | At the end of a few words: lie, die, pie, tie |
| /ō/ | oa, oe | boat, toe |
| not long or short | vowel r | An r after a vowel changes the sound of the vowel so that it is neither long nor short. far refer fir for fur |
| /ē/ | y | When y or ey ends a word in an unaccented syllable, it has the long sound of e. monkey |
| Long i | y | When y is at the end of a short word and is the only vowel, it has the long sound of i. my, shy fly |
| Long i | i | In a one syllable word with i as the only vowel, i before the final letters ld or nd is long. child, find |
| Long i<br>/ā/ | ie<br>ei | i before e except after c UNLESS they say a as in neighbor and weigh. |
| /ō/ | o | In a one syllable word with o as the only vowel, o before ld is long. bold, cold, hold, told |
| Silent e | e | e at the end of most words is silent. |
| /ow/ | ou | Use ou within a word. house |
| /ow/ | ow | Use ow at the end of a word (now) *Unless* ow is followed by l, n, or d. (except loud) howl, crown, crowd |
| /oi/ | oi | Use oi within a word. coil, toil |
| /oi/ | oy | Use oy at the end of a word. toy, boy |
| /oo/ | oo | oo says /oo/ in one syllable words. tool, food |
| /oo/ | u | u says /oo/ in words with more than one syllable, except blue. tulip, tuna, student |

## Reference Chart - Spelling Consonant Sounds

| *Sound* | *Spelling* | *Example* |
|---|---|---|
| /b/ | b | in box |
| | bb | in rabbit |
| /ch/ | ch | in chart |
| | tch | in catch |
| /d/ | d | in dime |
| | dd | in rudder |
| /dge/ | dge | in bridge |
| /f/ | f | in fun |
| | ff | in puff |
| | gh | in cough |
| | ph | in photo |
| /g/ | g | in g**a**te, g**o**, g**u**n |
| | gh | in ghost |
| /h/ | h | in hill |
| | wh | in who |
| /j/ | j | in jam |
| | g | in ag**e**, g**i**ant |
| | g | in g**y**m |
| /k/ | ch | in chorus |
| | ck | in back |
| | k | in lake |
| | c | in case |
| | que | in technique |
| /kw/ | qu | in quit |
| /l/ | ll | in mill |
| | le | in Bible |
| | el | in level |
| | l | in like |
| /w/ | w | in wing |
| | wh | in whistle |
| /ks/ | x | in box |
| /gz/ | x | in excite |
| /z/ | x | in xylophone |

| *Sound* | *Spelling* | *Example* |
|---|---|---|
| /m/ | m | in melt |
| | mb | in lamb |
| /n/ | nn | in banner |
| | n | in nice |
| | kn | in knee |
| | gn | in sign |
| /ng/ | n | in pink |
| | ng | in ring |
| /p/ | p | in pat |
| | pp | in happy |
| /r/ | r | in red |
| | rh | in rhyme |
| | rr | in berry |
| | wr | in wring |
| /s/ | s | in silk |
| | ss | in dress |
| | sc | in scene |
| | sw | in answer |
| | c | in face |
| /sh/ | s | in sugar |
| | ce | in ocean |
| | ch | in chauffeur |
| | ci | in special |
| /t/ | t | in time |
| | tt | in kitten, mitt |
| /th/ | th | in feather |
| | the | in bathe |
| /v/ | v | in vine |
| | ve | in cave |
| /y/ | y | in yarn |
| /z/ | z | in zebra |
| | ze | in freeze |
| | s | in is |
| | se | in noise |

# Reference Chart - Spelling Vowel Sounds

| *Sound* | *Spelling* | *Example* |
|---|---|---|
| Long a | a | in navy |
| | ai | in paid |
| | ay | in say |
| | ei | in veil |
| | eigh | in eight |
| a-consonant-e | | in gate |
| Long e | e | in he |
| | ea | in bead |
| | ee | in seed |
| | ei | in receive |
| | ey | in key |
| | y | in happy |
| | ie | in chief |
| e-consonant-e | | in these |
| Long i | i | in high |
| | ie | in tie |
| i-consonant-e | | in line |
| Long o | o | in hello |
| | oa | in coat |
| | oe | in toe |
| | ough | in though |
| o-consonant-e | | in vote |
| Long u | ew | in few |
| | ou | in you |
| | eu | in feud |
| u-consonant-e | | in mule |
| /ụ/ | oo | in foot |
| | u | in put |
| /aw/ | a | in hall |
| | au | in fault |
| | augh | in caught |
| | aw | in law |
| | ough | in thought |
| /er/ | er | in her |
| | ir | in sir |
| | or | in work |
| | ur | in nurse |

| *Sound* | *Spelling* | *Example* |
|---|---|---|
| /or/ | ar | in warm |
| | or | in horn |
| | our | in four |
| /ar/ | ar | in far |
| | ear | in heart |
| Short a | a | in cap |
| Short e | e | in get |
| | ea | in head |
| | ei | in forfeit |
| | ie | in friend |
| | a | in any |
| | ai | in said |
| | ay | in says |
| Short i | i | in hip |
| | ie | in sieve |
| | e | in pretty |
| | ee | in been |
| | u | in busy |
| | y | in mystery |
| Short o | o | in hot |
| | ow | in knowledge |
| Short u | u | in bus |
| | ou | in couple |
| /ow/ | ou | in shout |
| | ow | in how |
| /oi/ | oi | in foil |
| | oy | in toy |
| /oo/ | oo | in boot |
| | ew | in flew |
| | oe | in shoe |
| | ough | in through |
| | u | in tune |
| | ue | in blue |
| | ui | in fruit |

## Spelling Rules

### Plurals

*Although plural refers to nouns, the rules for adding s or es apply to verbs also.*

| **Add** | **When — Example** | |
|---|---|---|
| s | To form most plurals | cat - cats |
| | If the word ends in a vowel followed by y | key - keys |
| | To words ending in a vowel followed by o | radio - radios |
| | To words ending in a consonant followed by o that refer to music: alto - altos piano - pianos solo - solos and to a few others: twos, egos. Several words are correct with either s or es. | |
| | To most words ending in f (see "es' for exceptions) | |

| **Add** | **When — Example** |
|---|---|
| es | If the noun ends in ch, s, sh, x, or z<br>lunch*es* gas*es* brush*es* box*es* waltz*es* |
| | If the noun ends in consonant followed by a y, change y to i then add es. lady - ladies |
| | To some one-syllable nouns ending in a single f or fe, change f or fe to v when you can hear the v sound in the plural form, then add es. (Verb forms don't usually change).<br>leaf - leaves (noun); leafs (verb) |
| | To most words ending in a consonant followed by an o.<br>echo - echoes hero - heroes potato*es*, tomato*es*, torpedo*es* |

**Change the spelling** of some words rather than add s or es:

| | | |
|---|---|---|
| child - children | louse - lice | ox - oxen |
| foot - feet | man - men | tooth - teeth |
| goose - geese | mouse - mice | woman - women |

**Some words are the same** for both the singular and plural form:

bison deer grouse moose sheep swine

## Possessives

| Add | When | Example |
|---|---|---|
| 's | If the word does not end in s | boy's |
| ' | If the word ends in an s | boys' |
| nothing | To a personal pronoun | his, its, yours |

## Prefixes and Suffixes

| | |
|---|---|
| Prefixes | Add to the beginning of a word. No changes. *un*happy |
| Suffixes | Add to a word without changes unless there is a rule that applies: |
| Final c | If the suffix begins with e, i, or y, add a k after the letter c to prevent mispronunciation. picnic - picnicking |
| Final e | If a word ends in a silent e, drop the e when adding a suffix beginning with a vowel. (No changes for suffixes beginning with a consonant.)<br>**Except** When a word ends in ce or ge and the suffix begins with a or o, don't drop the final e.<br>peace - peaceable manage - manageable<br>*(See "Practicing the Rules" for a list of exceptions.)* |
| Final y | If the word ends in a consonant followed by y, change the y to i before adding endings that do not begin with i (ing, ist). (You do not want to write ii) carry - carrying - carried<br>(Keep the y if adding s to a proper name: *The Murphys*) |
| Doubling | Double the final consonant before adding a suffix that begins with a vowel if both of the following conditions are met:<br>1. The word has only one syllable or is accented on the last syllable with the accent remaining on that syllable once the suffix is added. |

2. The word ends in a single consonant preceded by a single vowel. **EXCEPT** when the final consonant is x, w, or y.

   pep - peppy    forget - forgetting

tion, sion

If a word ends in de, t, te, or se, drop those letters before adding tion or sion.    decide - decision    educate - education

EXCEPTIONS

A few words don't follow the rules and should be memorized:

| | | |
|---|---|---|
| argument | dyeing | dryly |
| judgment | hoeing | shyly |
| | singeing | slyly |
| acreage | shoeing | truly |
| lineage | skiing | wholly |
| mileage | | wryly |

Make a NOUN

Add one of the following suffixes to a base word to make a noun:    ian    ment    ness

| | | | | | |
|---|---|---|---|---|---|
| ar | ance | ist | ity | tion | ion |
| er | ence | | ty | ation | sion |
| or | | | y | | |

Make a VERB

Add one of the following suffixes to a base word to make a verb:

| | | | | | |
|---|---|---|---|---|---|
| ate | en | ify | ish | ize | ise |

Make an ADJECTIVE

Add one of the following suffixes to a base word to make an Adjective:

ly    ive    ful    ate

| | | | | | |
|---|---|---|---|---|---|
| able | al | ar | ary | ious | ous |
| ible | ial | iar | ery | eous | |

Make an ADVERB

Add one of the following suffixes to a base word to make an adverb:    ly    ily

Word Family: Words made from the same base word but with different prefixes and/or suffixes added:
base word: explode (verb)
nouns: explosion, explosive *(Dynamite is an explosive.)*
adjective: explosive *(Dynamite is an explosive device.)*
adverb: explosively

## Syllables

One syllable words — Do not divide one syllable words.

Compound Words — Many compound words are made from two one-syllable words. Divide the compound words into the two words from which it is made.

Affixes — Divide the word between the base or root word and the prefix and/or suffix (affixes). farm-er pre-view

Final le — Usually the consonant just before the le joins it.
sim-ple, sin-gle, hor-ri-ble

A Single Consonant — When a single consonant is between vowels, it usually goes with the second vowel. fa-mous ho-tel pi-lot

Double Consonants — Divide between double consonants that are in the middle of a word. rab-bit

Two Consonants — When the two consonants in the middle of a word make two sounds, divide between the two consonants.
af-ter gar-den mar-ket

Two Consonants — When the two consonants make one sound, do not divide them. pl in re-ply ch in re-searched
(Digraphs make one sound: sh ch th wh)

Hyphen — When coming to the end of a line requires dividing a word, always divide it after a syllable, using a hyphen. Don't divide it just before the last letter. There should be two or more letters at the end of a line and three or more letters at the beginning of a line.

## Writing Rules

### Capitalization

| | |
|---|---|
| First Words | Capitalize the first letter of the first word in a sentence.<br>Capitalize the first letter of the first word in each line of poetry.<br>Capitalize the first letter of the first word in each direct quotation. *John asked, "Where are you going?"* |
| Titles/Subtitles | Capitalize the first and all important words in a title.<br>*The Cat in the Hat. (Not a, an, the, to, and)* |
| I and O | Capitalize the letter I when it is used as the pronoun I.<br>Capitalize the interjection O. (Not oh.) |

Capitalize Proper Names and Proper Adjectives:

| | |
|---|---|
| Calendar Words | The first letter of each day of the week, month of the year, and each word naming a holiday. |
| Race - Nationality | Races, nationalities, and their languages.<br>*American, Caucasian, African-American, French, German* |
| Religion | The name of religious terms for the sacred.<br>scriptures - *the Bible (but not biblical), the Koran, the Torah*<br>deity - *God, Christ, Allah, Buddha.* (**He** *as the pronoun for deity*.)<br>The name of religions and their followers. *Christianity - Christians, Judaism - Orthodox Jew, Hinduism - Hindu* |
| Names | Important buildings and monuments *White House*<br>Specific persons<br>Specific places and geographical regions<br>country, state, city, province, *the South, the Northeast*<br>Historical events, Documents, Periods, Movements<br>*World War I, the Constitution, the Renaissance*<br>Organizations and their members. *Girl Scouts - Scout*<br>Trade names *Xerox, Ford* |

# Punctuation

| Use | | When |
|---|---|---|
| Colon | | Use a colon after a greeting in a business letter. |
| | | Use a colon to separate two independent clauses of a sentence when the second clause makes the first clause more clear. |
| Comma | Address: | Use between the city and the state. |
| | Adjective: | Separate two or more adjectives placed directly before the noun IF you could insert the word *and* without a change in meaning. *The large, hairy ape jumped.* |
| | Appositive: | Use commas to set off most appositives. *Jim, the athlete,...* |
| | Conjunction: | Use a comma before each of the following words in a compound sentence: *and, or, but, nor, for, so, yet* (That is, when they link main clauses, not when they link words or phrases: John *and* Jane sing. |
| | Date: | Use between the day and the year. *June 4, 1912* |
| | Direct Address: | Set off a noun in direct address: *Come here, John.* |
| | Letter: | Use after the greeting in a friendly letter. Use after the closing in any letter. |
| | Parenthetical Expressions | are usually set off by commas. These are explanatory, supplementary, or transitional words or phrases. |
| | Quotation: | At the end of a sentence and inside quotation marks when it is not the finish of the sentence. *"I'll help," said Jane.* |
| | Series: | Separate three or more items in a list (series) in a sentence. |
| Comma | | Place a comma after the following when they begin a sentence: Words: Yes, No, However, Well, Of course, Therefore, For example. Mild Interjections: *Goodness*, what a mess! |

Adverbial Clause: *After the movie*, we'll go to dinner.

| | |
|---|---|
| Exclamation Point: | Use after an exclamatory sentence. |
| | Use after a strong interjection. |
| Period | A period indicates a full stop at the end of a sentence. |
| | Use at the end of a declarative or an imperative sentence. |
| | Use after most abbreviations, including initials. Some acceptable exceptions: TV, UN, AM, FM, rpm, kg, km (et. al.) |
| | Use after a Roman numeral numbering the main topic in an outline. |
| | Use after a letter noting a sub-topic in an outline. |
| Question Mark | Place at the end of an interrogative sentence. |
| | Use quotation marks to denote minor titles: songs, articles, short stories, minor poems, chapters in books. |
| | Place quotation marks directly before and after each direct quotation, and only around the quoted words. Punctuation is placed inside the quotation marks. |
| Semicolon | Use to separate two independent clauses |
| | Use a semicolon to separate a series made up of long and complex phrases. |
| Underline (or italicize) | Titles of works that appear independently: books, plays, long poems published as books, pamphlets, newspapers, works of visual art, magazines, published speeches, record albums, musical compositions, movies, television and radio programs. |
| | Names of aircraft, ships, spacecraft, and trains. |
| | Foreign words and phrases not used as part of English, including the Latin scientific names for plants and animals. |

## Common Affixes and Their Meanings

### Prefixes

*Prefixes are attached to a word without changes to the base word.*

semi + annual = semiannual

Note: Many words enter English with the prefix already attached. (e.g. anarchy, excel)

*Prefixes change the meaning of a word.* read - reread (read again)

| Prefix | Meaning | Example |
|---|---|---|
| a | at, on, in | abed |
| a, an | without, not | atheist |
| ab | away from, off | absent |
| ad | to, toward | adjoin |
| anti, ob | against | antibody |
| com, con | with, together | compress |
| de | away from, reverse of | devalue |
| dis | apart, opposite of | disagree |
| dis | lacking in, not | disprove |
| en | in, into, cause to be | engage |
| ex, e | out of, from | extrude |
| im, in | not | impossible |
| ir, il | not | illiterate |
| in | in, on , into, toward | intrude |
| inter | between, among | interstate |
| intra | within | intramural |
| mis | badly, wrongly | misprint |
| non, un | not | nonstop |
| out | out | outcast |
| over | above, beyond, over | overpaid |

*Prefixes*

| ***Prefix*** | ***Meaning*** | ***Example*** |
|---|---|---|
| post | after, behind | postscript |
| pre | before | prepay |
| pro | for, in place of | proclaim |
| re | again, or backward | reappear |
| semi | half | semicircle |
| super | above, beyond | supersonic |
| trans | across | transcend |
| un | not | unbelievable |
| under | below, beneath, lower | underfed |

**Number Prefixes (Latin)**

| | | |
|---|---|---|
| uni | one | unicycle |
| bi | two | bicycle |
| tri | three | triplets |
| quad | four | quadruplets |
| quin | five | quintuplets |
| hex | six | hexagon |
| hep | seven | heptagon |
| oct | eight | octagon |
| deca | ten | decade |
| cent | hundred | century |
| mil | thousand | millennium |

## Suffixes

*Suffixes change the part of speech of a word. For example, the noun* love *is changed to an adjective with the addition of* ly - lovely.

OR *suffixes indicate the plural form* (s, es, ies), *a form of a verb* (swims), *or the tense*:

Past Tense - *ed*
Present participle - *ing*
Comparative or Superlative degree - *er, est*

*Suffixes*

| **Suffix** | **Meaning** | **Example** |
| --- | --- | --- |
| able, ible | able to | enjoyable |
| ary, ery, ory | related to | judiciary |
| ation | act of | narration |
| dom | rank, domain | kingdom |
| en | consisting of, like | wooden |
| er, or | one who | teacher |
| ess | female | lioness |
| ful | full of, amount needed | beautiful |
| ic | having the character of | heroic |
| ic | associated with | mechanic |
| ice, ise, ize | to make or become | mechanize |
| less | unable, not having | childless |
| ly | per, like | kindly |
| ness | state or condition of | kindness |
| ous | full of, having | poisonous |
| y | like, quality of | sticky |

Add a suffix to a base word to make a noun:
ar, er, or    ence, ance    ian    ity, ty, y    ment
ness    ation, ion, sion, tion    al

Add a suffix to a base word to make a verb:
ate    en    ify    ish    ize, ise, ice

Add a suffix to a base word to make an adjective:
able, ible    ly    al, ial    ar, iar    ary, ery    ful    ous, ious, eous

Add a suffix to a base word to make an adverb: ly

PRACTICE adding prefixes and suffixes to make a word family. Also practice adding the most common endings. s, es, ies    ed    ing    er, est

fix: fixes, fixed, fixing
fast: fast, faster, fastest
kind: unkind, kindly, kindness
teach: teaches, teacher, teachable
response: responsive, responsible, irresponsible

# Practicing the Rules

## Vowel Sounds / Grades 1-3

*The two most useful rules are:*

1. In one syllable words with a single vowel in the middle, the vowel has the short sound. (clap, pet, fix, mop, nut )

2. When the last three letters of a word are a single vowel followed by a consonant and an *e*, the vowel has the long sound. (late, hope, vine, note, mute )

*To review these rules, show the student how adding a final, and silent, letter e changes the vowel sound of the word:*

| | | | | | |
|---|---|---|---|---|---|
| bit | bite | hop | hope | rat | rate |
| can | cane | man | mane | rid | ride |
| far | fare | not | note | rip | ripe |
| fin | fine | pin | pine | shin | shine |
| hid | hide | plan | plane | slid | slide |

## Adding s, es, ies / Grades 1-6

Plural refers to nouns, but verbs follow these rules when adding *s* also.

1. **Add *s* to most words** including:

- Words that end in a vowel followed by the letter *y*: toy - toys

| | | | |
|---|---|---|---|
| betray | day | galley | key |
| play | donkey | highway | monkey |
| chimney | employ | journey | railway |
| convey | enjoy | joy | turkey |

- Most words ending in *f*.

 **Except** a few **nouns** that end in *f* or *fe* that change the *f* or *fe* to *v* and add *es*. You can hear the *v* sound when you say the plural.

*Examples:*

| | | | | |
|---|---|---|---|---|
| calf | calves | | loaf | loaves |
| elf | elves | | self | selves |
| half | halves | | shelf | shelves |
| knife | knives | (verb: knifes) | thief | thieves |
| leaf | leaves | (verb: leafs) | wife | wives |
| life | lives | | wolf | wolves |

*A few words can use* s *or* ves*:* scarf, hoof, wharf. *Since they allow a choice, it is easier to memorize the list above and just add s to all others.*

- Words that end in an *o* preceded by a consonant if the word refers to music, and a few other words: altos pianos solos twos egos

Note: Many words ending in *o* can be spelled correctly in both forms—with an *s* or an *es*. *(See page 83.)*

2. **Add *es*** in the following cases:

- Add *es* if the word ends in *ch, s, sh, x, z*
  *This also applies to verbs when spelling the third person singular.*

| **ch** | **s** |
|---|---|
| bench - benches | bus - buses |
| brunch - brunches | circus - circuses |
| catch - catches | compass - compasses |
| lunch - lunches | cross - crosses |
| switch - switches | dress - dresses |
| torch - torches | gas - gases |
| twitch - twitches | glass - glasses |
| watch - watches | press - presses |

| **sh** | **x** | **z** |
|---|---|---|
| bush*es* | affix*es* | buzz*es* |
| brush*es* | box*es* | fizz*es* |
| cherish*es* | fix*es* | frizz*es* |
| crush*es* | relax*es* | *quiz *zes* |
| nourish*es* | reflex*es* | *whiz *zes* |
| rush*es* | six*es* | waltz*es* |
| wash*es* | suffix*es* | |
| wish*es* | tax*es* | |

*(*Refer to Adding suffixes, rule #5, page 85)*

- Add *es* if the noun or verb ends in a consonant followed by a *y*. Change the *y* to *i*, then add *es*.

| | | | |
|---|---|---|---|
| baby - babies | dry - dries | occupy - occupies | salary - salaries |
| battery - batteries | forty - forties | pity - pities | sky - skies |
| buggy - buggies | hobby - hobbies | policy - policies | story - stories |
| bunny - bunnies | marry - marries | pony - ponies | theory - theories |
| carry - carries | notify - notifies | puppy - puppies | try - tries |

- Add es to most words ending in a consonant followed by o *(except words referring to music which add s.)*

| | | | | | |
|---|---|---|---|---|---|
| echo*es* | hero*es* | potato*es* | torpedo*es* | *Verbs:* | do - does |
| embargo*es* | no*es* | tomato*es* | veto*es* | | go - goes |

Some words are correct with either an s or an es added: tornado, buffalo, motto, zero, volcano, calico, halo, domino, tobacco, cargo, proviso, innuendo.

*3.* **Change the spelling of some words** rather than adding an *s* or an *es.*

| | | |
|---|---|---|
| child - children | louse - lice | ox - oxen |
| foot - feet | man - men | tooth - teeth |
| goose - geese | mouse - mice | woman - women |

4. Some words **stay the same** for both the singular and plural form:

deer grouse moose sheep swine

## Suffixes / Grades 1-8

Add a suffix without any changes to the base word ***unless*** the word fits into one of the following categories:

1. If the word ends in the letter *c* add a *k* before any suffix beginning with *e, i,* or *y.*

frolic - frolicking mimic - mimicking picnic - picnicking

2. If a word ends in a consonant followed by a *y*, change the *y* to ***i*** **unless** the suffix begins with an *i*. *(ing, ist: You do not want to write ii except in skiing.)*

| | | | | |
|---|---|---|---|---|
| *beauty* | beautiful | beautifully | beautician | |
| *bury* | buries | buried | (burying) | |
| *carry* | carries | carried | carriage | (carrying) |
| *comedy* | comedies | comedian | | |
| *duty* | dutiful | dutifully | | |
| *envy* | envious | enviable | envies | |
| *happy* | happily | happiness | | |
| *library* | libraries | | | |
| *lullaby* | lullabies | | | |

3. If a word ends in a silent *e*, drop the *e* before adding a suffix that begins with a vowel. **Except** if the word ends in *ce* or *ge* and the suffix begins with *a* or *o*. In that case, keep the *e*.

*Suffixes:* able, ible, er, or, ar, ian, an, ist, est, en, ous, ify, ish, ize, ise, ice, ive, ate, ary, ery, ing, y

| | |
|---|---|
| *fame* | famous |
| *motive* | motivate, motivation |
| *nerve* | nervous, nervy |
| *please* | pleasant, pleasing |
| *reverse* | reversible |
| *rose* | rosy |
| *store* | storage |
| *tickle* | ticklish |

*Words ending in* ce *or* ge

| | | | |
|---|---|---|---|
| *embrace* | embraceable | *change* | changeable |
| *peace* | peaceable | *manage* | manageable |
| *trace* | traceable | *outrage* | outrageous |

**Exceptions:**

| | |
|---|---|
| *acre* | acreage |
| *hoe* | hoeing |
| *line* | lineage |
| *mile* | mileage |
| *shoe* | shoeing |

3. If a word ends in *de, t, te,* or *se,* drop those letters before adding *tion* or *sion.* *(Grades 4-8)*

| | | | |
|---|---|---|---|
| *decide* | decision | *communicate* | communication |
| *divide* | division | *educate* | education |
| *provide* | provision | *graduate* | graduation |
| *act* | action | *confuse* | confusion |
| *instruct* | instruction | *infuse* | infusion |
| *protect* | protection | *repulse* | *repulsion* |

4. A few words have two correct spellings:

| | | |
|---|---|---|
| bony / boney | likable / likeable | movable / moveable |
| homy / homey | lovable / loveable | sizable / sizeable |
| lacy / lacey | mousy / mousey | usable / useable |

5. *Doubling:* Double the final consonant of a word before adding a suffix that begins with a vowel (including y) IF the word is one syllable, or the stress is on the last syllable and remains on that syllable after a suffix is added, AND the word ends in a single vowel followed by a single consonant, UNLESS the final consonant is *x, w,* or *y.*

(refer - referring - reference. *When* ence *is added the stress does not stay on the last syllable of the base word, therefore the final r is not doubled.)*

| | |
|---|---|
| *drug* | drugged, druggist |
| *forgot* | forgotten, (forgetting) |
| *glad* | gladden |
| *hop* | hopping, hopped |
| *hot* | hotter, hottest |
| *omit* | omitted, omitting |
| *pep* | peppy |
| *propel* | propeller, propelled, propelling |
| *quit** | quitter, quitted, quitting |
| *quiz** | quizzes, quizzed (*qu acts as a consonant, leaving i as a single vowel) |
| *rebel* | rebellion |
| *regret* | regrettable, regretted |
| *swim* | swimmer, swimming |
| *shop* | shopper, shopped, shopping |
| *zip* | zipped |

## Friendly Letter Format

*Note margins, capital letters, and commas.*

**HEADING**

Your Street Address
Your City, State and zip code
Month and date, year

Dear Name, **SALUTATION** *(Greeting)*

**BODY**

Indent the first line of the letter and the first line of each paragraph. Line up the other lines with the left margin established by your greeting. If you are typing the letter, space in five spaces, then start typing. At the end of a sentence, leave two spaces before typing the next sentence.

In a friendly letter there are no spaces between the paragraphs. The indentation is enough to signal the change.

Notice that the closing and signature are lined up with the left margin of the heading. The heading is started about halfway across the paper. When typing a letter, type the closing but not the name of the author. A personal signature alone is all that is necessary.

Leave two lines between the heading and greeting, between the greeting and the body, and between the body and the closing if the letter is typed. No extra lines are necessary if it is handwritten, but may be added for a better appearance.

Remember to use a comma between the city and state, the date and year (March 12, 1989, for example) and after the greeting and closing. Notice that in a friendly letter the greeting uses the person's name rather than Sir.

The name of your street, city, and state as well as the month, the greeting, and the closing each begin with a capital letter.

**CLOSING** — Sincerely,

**SIGNATURE** — *Your Name*

**ENVELOPE**

Your Name
Your Street Address
Your City, State, & zip code

Stamp

First and Last Name of person in greeting
Street Address of the person in the greeting
City, State and zip code

## Business Letter - Semi-Block Format

*Pay attention to margins, capital letters, commas, and colons.*

**HEADING**

Your Street Address
Your City, State and zip code
Month and date, year

Name of Business
Street Address
City, State and zip code

**INSIDE ADDRESS**

Dear Sir or Madam: **SALUTATION** ***(Greeting)***

**BODY**

The greeting is always formal and is followed by a colon. If you know the name of the person, use his or her title (Dr., Professor).

A comma separates city and state, but not state and zip code. A comma separates the year from the month and date.

Notice that there are several lines between the heading and the inside address. There are two lines between the inside address and the greeting, between the greeting and the first sentence of the letter, and between the end of the letter and the closing. Leave four lines between the closing and the typed name of the writer. The hand-signed signature of the first and last name goes in that space. Do not add Mr. or Mrs. to the signature.

Indent five spaces to begin each paragraph and do not leave space between paragraphs.

The heading begins about halfway across the page. The closing and typed name of the writer should line up with the left margin of the heading.

The entire letter should be centered on the page with the same margin on the left and right and at least an inch at the top and bottom for best appearance.

The closing is formal. Most common choices are *Very truly yours*, *Sincerely yours*, or simply, *Sincerely*.

**CLOSING** Sincerely,

**SIGNATURE**

*Personal signature*

Typed name of author

## Business Letter - Block Format

Your Street Address
Your City, State and zip code
Today's Date

**HEADING**

Name of Business
Street Address of Business
City, State and zip code

**INSIDE ADDRESS**

Dear Sir or Madam:

**SALUTATION** *(Greeting)*

**BODY**

There are no indentations for paragraphs. Line up the heading, inside address, salutation, body of the letter, and closing with the left margin. Leave a line of space between the heading and inside address, between the inside address and the greeting, and between the greeting and the first line of the body. (Press *Return* or *Enter* twice if typing.)

Leave a line of space between each paragraph. At the end of the letter, leave a line and then write the closing. (Press *Return* or *Enter* twice if typing.)

After the closing, leave three lines of space, typing the name of the author on the fourth line. (Press *Return* or *Enter* four times.) A personal signature, first and last name, should be written by hand in that space.

For best appearance, the letter should be centered on the page with equal margins on the left and right and at least an inch margin on the top and bottom.

Sincerely,

**CLOSING**

*Personal Signature*

Typed name of author

**SIGNATURE**

## Dictionary Page - Sample

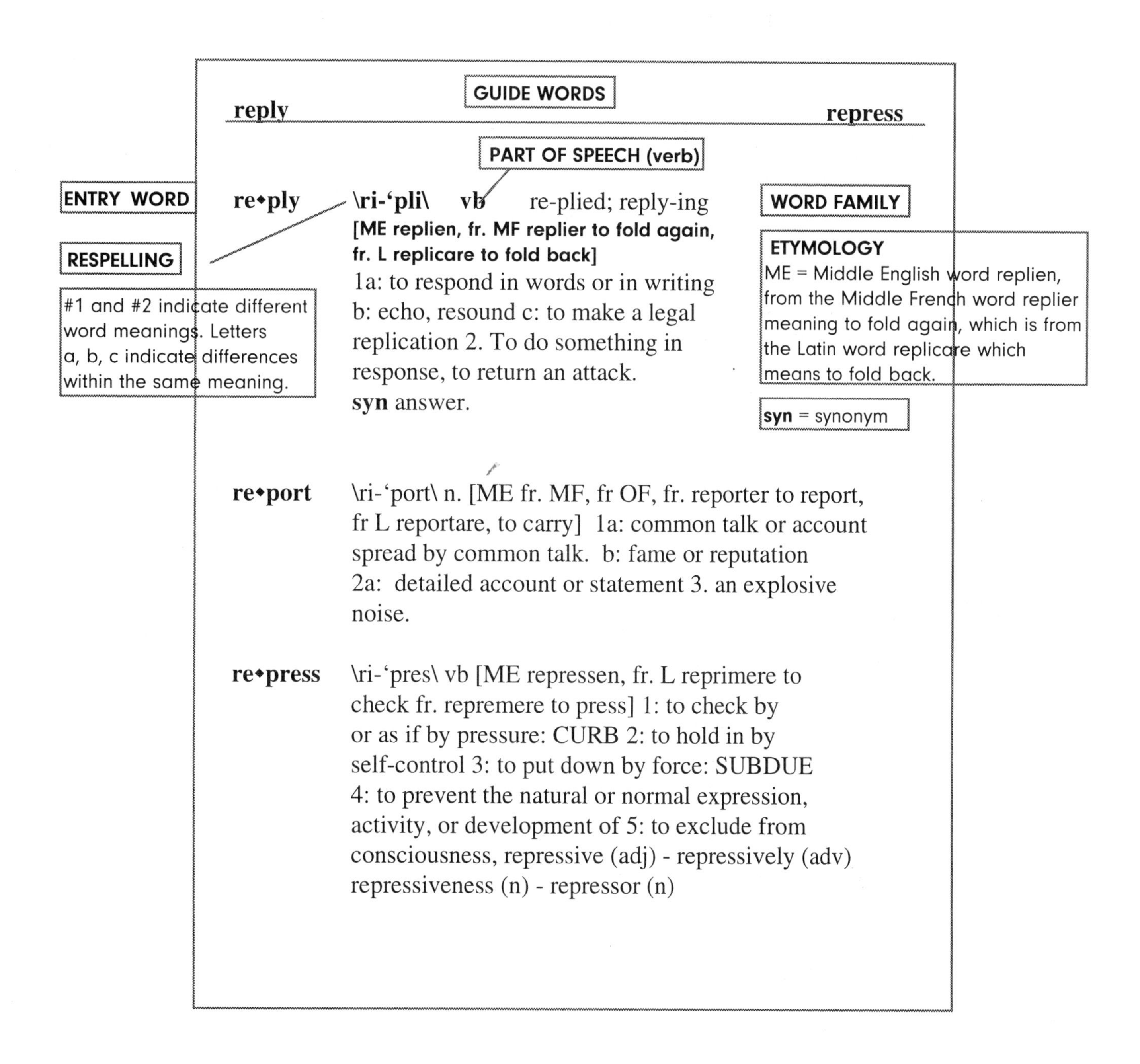

GUIDE WORDS
reply
repress
PART OF SPEECH (verb)
ENTRY WORD
re•ply
\ri-'pli\ vb re-plied; reply-ing
[ME replien, fr. MF replier to fold again, fr. L replicare to fold back]
1a: to respond in words or in writing b: echo, resound c: to make a legal replication 2. To do something in response, to return an attack.
syn answer.
WORD FAMILY
RESPELLING
#1 and #2 indicate different word meanings. Letters a, b, c indicate differences within the same meaning.
ETYMOLOGY
ME = Middle English word replien, from the Middle French word replier meaning to fold again, which is from the Latin word replicare which means to fold back.
syn = synonym
re•port
\ri-'port\ n. [ME fr. MF, fr OF, fr. reporter to report, fr L reportare, to carry] 1a: common talk or account spread by common talk. b: fame or reputation 2a: detailed account or statement 3. an explosive noise.
re•press
\ri-'pres\ vb [ME repressen, fr. L reprimere to check fr. repremere to press] 1: to check by or as if by pressure: CURB 2: to hold in by self-control 3: to put down by force: SUBDUE 4: to prevent the natural or normal expression, activity, or development of 5: to exclude from consciousness, repressive (adj) - repressively (adv) repressiveness (n) - repressor (n)


*(Entries taken in part from Webster's Seventh New Collegiate Dictionary, G&C Merriam Company, 1967)*

# GLOSSARY OF TERMS

**Abbreviation** A shortened form of a word. *Mr. for Mister*

**Adjective** A word that gives more information about (modifies) a noun. House is a noun. Big is an adjective: *big house.* It tells what—what kind, what color, what size, and so on, and how many: *two houses.*

**Adverb** A word that gives more information about (modifies) a verb (run quickly), adjective (quite funny), or another adverb (very quickly).

**Antonyms** Words that have opposite meanings: light-dark

**Base word** A word before any changes have been made. *Walk is the base word of walking.*

**Closed syllable** A syllable that ends with a consonant sound. *Hon-est: both hon and est are closed syllables.*

**Compound Word** A noun or adjective formed from two or more words. *Baseball is a compound of base and ball.*

**Consonant** Letters of the alphabet other than the letters a, e, i, o, and u

**Consonant Cluster** Sounds that come together in a word. *st in stamp, str in street, pr in pray*

**Consonant Sound** The sound made when pronouncing the consonants and not the vowels in a word.

**Contraction** A shortened form of a word or words. An apostrophe (') indicates the place where a letter or letters have been left out.

**Dictionary Skills** Demonstrating the knowledge of the meaning or use of entry words, guide words, alphabetical order, syllabication, accent or stress on syllables, phonetic respelling, pronunciation guide, various meanings of a word, word history or etymology, part of speech of the word.

**Digraph** Two letters that spell a single sound. *ch in chair, sh in shy, th in thumb*

**Double Letters** Two of the same letters next to each other in a word. *rubber dollar staff*

**Entry word** A word in the dictionary which is followed by a definition.

**Etymology** The history of a word. That is, the language and meaning from which the word originated.

**Guide Words** The two words at the top of a dictionary page. These are the first and last words defined on the page.

**Heteronyms** Words that are spelled the same but are pronounced differently and have different meanings.

**Homonyms** Strictly speaking, they are words that have the same spelling, the same pronunciation, but different meanings. However, it is often used to describe homophones—words which sound alike but are spelled differently.

**Homophones** Words that sound the same but have different meanings and/or spellings.

**Long Vowel** The sound of a, e, i, o, and u in the words late, Pete, kite, mote, and cute. (The letter sounds like its name.)

**Noun** A word for a person, place or thing. *(girl, city, cup)*

**Open Compound Word** A compound word written as separate words. post office, town hall

**Open Syllable** A syllable that ends in a vowel sound. Stu-dent: the syllable stu ends in a vowel sound.

**Part-of-speech label** An abbreviation in a dictionary that tells the part of speech of each entry word. n. noun, v. verb, adj. adjective, adv. adverb, pron. pronoun, prep. preposition, conj. conjunction, interj. Interjection

**Phonetics** Representing each speech sound with a particular symbol.

**Phonetic Respelling** Spelling a word according to phonic generalizations for each syllable. *Photo = foh toh*

**Phonics** Using sound to teach reading.

**Plural** A word that stands for more than one of something. *Toy is singular (one) and toys is the plural form.*

**Possessive** A form of a word that shows ownership. *Joe's car*

**Prefix** A syllable or syllables added to the beginning of a base word or root. *kind: unkind, un is a prefix*

**Pronunciation** How to say a word is shown in the dictionary using phonetic spellings, symbols, and accent marks. *red'-i-lee for readily.*

**Pronunciation Key** A chart in the dictionary lists a symbol used for each sound in the pronunciation respelling listed next to each entry word.

**Respelling** The phonetic spelling that follows a dictionary entry word to be used as a guide to correct pronunciation. */kōm/ for comb*

**Root Word** Parts that do not usually stand alone in English, but are words when a prefix or suffix is added. *pend - meaning to hang: depend, dependent.*

**Short Vowel** The sound of a, e, i, o, and u in the words *ran, hen, pin, pond*, and *sun*.

**Stress Mark** The mark (') used in dictionary respellings to indicate which syllable is said with greater force. *co' zy*

**Suffix** A letter or letters added to the end of a word. *ly is a suffix. sad - sadly.*

**Syllable** A word or a part of a word with one vowel sound. *Smell has one syllable. Slo and gan are each syllables in slogan.*

**Synonyms** Words that have the same or almost the same meaning. *Happy and glad are synonyms.*

**Verb** A word that indicates action or a state of being. *run, skip, think* Forms of to be indicate being*: am, is, are, was, were (etcetera)*

**Vowel Sound** A sound that is usually spelled with one or more of these letters: a, e, i, o, u, y

**Word Family** Words based on the same base or root word, but with various beginnings and endings added on. *joy: joyful, joyous, joyfully, enjoy*

**Word history** The words in brackets in a dictionary entry which indicate the language and meaning of the word's origin. Also called etymology. Dictionaries use abbreviations for the language such as ME for Middle English, F for French, L for Latin, and Gk for Greek.

**Word Meaning** The understanding of the meaning of a word can come from several sources: clues in a picture accompanying the text (grades 1-7), the context in which the word is used (grades 2-8), the definition listed in a dictionary (grades 3-8), deductive reasoning based on the knowledge of the meaning of various word parts—prefix, suffix, root word, words in a compound word. (grades 4-8)